D1540151

Principals of
Dynamic Schools

A joint publication of
The National Association of Secondary School Principals
and
Corwin Press, Inc.

Principals of Dynamic Schools

TAKING CHARGE OF CHANGE

✳✳✳✳✳

Ellen B. Goldring
Sharon F. Rallis

CORWIN PRESS, INC.
A Sage Publications Company
Newbury Park, California

Copyright © 1993 by Corwin Press, Inc.

All rights reserved. No part of this book may be reproduced or utilized in any form or by any means, electronic or mechanical, including photocopying, recording, or by any information storage and retrieval system, without permission in writing from the publisher.

For information address:

Corwin Press, Inc.
A Sage Publications Company
2455 Teller Road
Newbury Park, California 91320

SAGE Publications Ltd.
6 Bonhill Street
London EC2A 4PU
United Kingdom

SAGE Publications India Pvt. Ltd.
M-32 Market
Greater Kailash I
New Delhi 110 048 India

Printed in the United States of America

Library of Congress Cataloging-in-Publication Data

Goldring, Ellen B. (Ellen Borish), 1957-
    Principals of dynamic schools : taking charge of change / Ellen B.
Goldring, Sharon F. Rallis.
        p. cm.
    Includes bibliographical references (pp. 151-168) and index.
    ISBN 0-8039-6067-0 (cloth)—ISBN 0-8039-6068-9 (pbk.)
    1. School principals—United States. 2. School management and
organization—United States. 3. Educational leadership—United
States. I. Rallis, Sharon F. II. Title.
LB2831.92.G65 1993
371.2'012'0973—dc20   93-15409
                                                                  CIP

93 94 95 10 9 8 7 6 5 4 3 2 1

Corwin Press Production Editor: Tara S. Mead

Contents

Foreword

This is a welcome book. Ellen Goldring and Sharon Rallis provide a lively and inspiring view of school leadership that is both grounded in reality and compellingly hopeful that this reality can be redefined for the better. *Principals of Dynamic Schools* packs more useful ideas about what leadership is and how it works in successfully restructuring schools than any other book now available. And the authors speak to this topic with a voice that is as passionate and sensitive as it is reasoned and authoritative.

The reader should beware, however. We educators have a history of taking new ideas and understanding them in the terms of existing categories. When this happens our old theories are dressed up a little but remain unchanged. For this reason some readers who are fearful of fundamental changes will find references to "the dynamic school" and to "principal-in-charge" reassuring and comforting. They may see this book as another in a long series designed to offer ideas aimed at improving schools by getting our old theories to work better. We've often been through this kind of counterfeit redefinition with few sustained changes for the better. The principal as the instructional leader of the school who "progressively" empowers teachers by letting them share in the decision-making process is a recent example. Within this view, *principal-in-charge* means keeping the principal at the center as the one who provides the vision and lays out the expectations and then who practices the right blend of management and human relations to get the job done. The idea is to get teachers to do what it is that the principal wants and have them enjoy it at the same time. Because so much of what happens in this old theory rests on the shoulders of principals, they are prone to borrow or buy their visions and expectations from "experts" by importing packaged approaches to school improvement. Most packages have appeal because they reinforce the old theory by accommodating the idea of the principal being at the center of everything.

Goldring and Rallis tell another story. Relying on their own ambitious and extensive case studies and survey studies and on a thorough overview of the research of others, they define anew what it means for principals to be in charge. The principals they studied were much less concerned with controlling what people did and how they did it and much more concerned with controlling the conditions that enabled others to function in ways that increased the likelihood shared goals would be reached. They had power and were not afraid to use it to make others powerful, to remove obstacles, to create the conditions of success. Their practices were characterized by conviction and caring as well as a sense of the practical and real. They realized that bringing about enough consensus to make things work and to enable people to become self-managing and -leading means that the school must commit itself to inventing its own practice. And this commitment is manifested in collective inquiry and problem solving. These principals were very much in charge but differently in charge. They were leaders in the truest sense of the word. They took their stewardship responsibility seriously. They placed themselves in service to ideas and to those who were working to make these ideas a reality. And as a result they increased the importance and significance of the principalship.

Principals of Dynamic Schools is a practical book, richly written in plain English. And it is a scholarly book for the same reasons. With its publication, Goldring and Rallis move to the head of the line of scholars who are struggling to redefine how leadership works in restructuring schools. I recommend it without qualification.

THOMAS J. SERGIOVANNI
Trinity University

Preface

Leadership has been a popular topic in journals, how-to books, and educational reform literature. Although new visions of the school principal as leader are emerging, few address the new roles required of them in the changing educational environment. The reform agenda is creating new configurations in schools that force principals to adapt. These new configurations include teacher-leaders, parent advocates, expanded communities and services, diverse student bodies, and external regulations. This book, meshing past research with new data, synthesizes a new vision of the principalship. We explore the evolution of the principal's role in the context of the changing school. We dub these new leaders *principals-in-charge*.

The term *principal-in-charge* may invoke the image of the old-time bureaucratic leader, sitting at the top of the hierarchical school organization. This is not our intent. Throughout this book, our image of the principal-in-charge is that of a collaborative principal, working toward change, taking charge and coordinating school activities. Weighing the complexities of the role and the enormous pressures on schools today, the principal must be strong and in charge. We see no tension between the principal who is collaborating and coordinating while also taking charge and being accountable. This book introduces Lee Palmer, the principal-in-charge of Vibrant Springs School, a dynamic school. From Lee, we learn about the leadership style of principals-in-charge, and we see why Lee is the principal of a dynamic school. Lee's actions shape an emerging conceptualization of principals within the changing school context. A glimpse of Lee's professional life offers insight into the ways the principal responds to the novel and complex forces that carry new demands and expectations for schools and school leaders. Because Lee is a composite of the various principals we have seen, we recognize that this leader may appear larger than life. Lee's every thought and action, however, derive from at least one practicing principal in our data base.

Overview of the Book

This volume explores the new roles that principals of dynamic schools encounter. We describe and illustrate the behavior of these new principals and the forces that shape their activities. The first chapter examines the following forces as shaping the principal-in-charge:

- Teachers are becoming teacher-leaders.
- Parents are more vocal and action-oriented advocates.
- Student bodies are more diverse with a variety of needs.
- The social and technological contexts of schools are more complex.
- State and federal reform mandates are setting priorities.

The second chapter develops the image of a dynamic school as the place where principals-in-charge work and introduces the characteristics that define this type of principal.

The following three chapters examine new roles for principals-in-charge: *facilitating, balancing,* and *flag bearing.* Chapter 3 discusses the professional relationships that principals-in-charge develop to facilitate teachers in dynamic schools. These are teachers who are empowered to carry out many of the tasks previously delegated to the principal. Initially by giving teachers room to create and then by coordinating the various programs, principals-in-charge facilitate students becoming active learners in a creative, productive school environment.

Chapter 4 develops the role of the principal-in-charge negotiating within the system hierarchy. Principals-in-charge strike a balance between independence and control in the system hierarchy. This chapter discusses the methods principals-in-charge use to develop mutual, cooperative relationships with their superiors.

Chapter 5 presents the principal-in-charge as the flag bearer and bridger: Principals-in-charge take on the role of entrepreneur for the school in the community. This chapter discusses the principal as the enterprising external leader who crosses the boundaries between school and community to develop and nourish support and to mobilize resources.

In the next two chapters, we offer new approaches to assessing and preparing the principal-in-charge. In Chapter 6, we suggest that our new image of a principal carries major consequences for assessing principals and schools. Dynamic schools are evaluation-minded schools (Nevo, 1991) with a commitment to collective problem solving. Assessments are conducted from a school-based approach in which the principal plays a crucial role.

Chapter 7 discusses the leadership development needs of principals-in-charge. Principals, if they are to be in charge, require new preparation programs and alternative modes for development. This chapter provides a prospectus for such programs and discusses methods for enabling principals to maintain their momentum of continuous growth.

The concluding chapter offers the role of principals-in-charge as leaders of change. Schools that have principals-in-charge are, as we have defined them, changed schools. This chapter contributes to the ongoing discussion about the importance of principals in promoting and sustaining change in schools. We argue that to have changed schools, schools must have principals-in-charge.

Each chapter follows a similar design. We introduce a scenario with Lee Palmer, our principal-in-charge of a dynamic school, who exemplifies the leadership properties that we portray in that chapter. Empirical data and supporting literature then illustrate and validate the leadership characteristic. Last, we summarize the chapter by highlighting the central aspects of the theme.

Knowledge Bases

The two of us bring to this project very different experiences and strengths. Goldring has an academic orientation with skills and experience in quantitative data analysis. For years she has studied principals as well as their relationships with parents and the community. Rallis has a stronger practice orientation, having spent years as a teacher, a school principal, and later as a program developer and evaluator in schools. The discovery that we had captured some of the same phenomena in our separate bodies of research led to our collaboration. Rallis was fascinated that Goldring's conclusions, drawn from analyses of survey data, matched her own conclusions from analyses of case studies and interviews. Similarly, Goldring was encouraged that Rallis's studies corroborated the quantitative findings. Specifically, we both observed that some schools exemplified the characteristics of what we call dynamic schools, whereas others did not. Simultaneously, we recognized the presence of a principal who behaved in certain ways as leader in these dynamic schools.

Our conceptualization of the principal-in-charge is thus based on the synthesis of several systematic, yet complementary, inquiries. To develop the image of the principal-in-charge and to portray both breadth and depth of these principals, we have synthesized and drawn from a number of sources, including the qualitative and quantitative analyses of principals and the literature from the fields of education, organizations, and leadership. The bodies of knowledge used to paint the portrait of the principal-in-charge include detailed reports of unique dynamic schools and in-depth analyses of principals engaged in change as well as analyses of large-scale survey data revealing trends in the new roles of principals today. The case studies offer rich detail of the leadership styles of principals-in-charge, whereas the survey data provide a view of the scope of the phenomenon.

To advance our image of the principal-in-charge, Rallis brings data drawn from three studies: (1) a 5-year evaluation of the Classroom Alternative Process (CAP), a federally funded state-wide initiative to establish building-based problem-solving teams in schools (Rallis, 1989); (2) a 2-year study of eight schools that had adopted the least restrictive environment (LRE) initiative, a feder-ally supported effort to integrate students with disabilities into regular education classrooms (Rallis, 1991); and (3) an in-depth case study of a principal in a Coalition of Essential Schools (Coali-tion) high school (Rallis, 1992). The Coalition is a network of schools, primarily secondary schools, that collaborate and sup-port each other as they implement the Nine Common Principles presented in *Horace's Compromise* (Sizer, 1984). The difficulties all these principals encountered illustrate the magnitude and complex-ity of leading a dynamic school. To illustrate the scope of our image, Goldring brings analyses of the Administrator Survey from the *High School and Beyond* data set (U.S. Department of Education, 1984). (See Appendix for specific details of all of these studies.) These studies of principals, supported by our years of work in schools, portray the principal-in-charge that we present in the following pages.

Acknowledgments

We are grateful to many people for their help in the creation of this volume. At Vanderbilt, we thank our graduate students Joy Criscoe, Charles Hausman, Kathy Martin, and Anna Sullivan for their hours of searching, editing, proofing, and commenting. We also thank Mike Shackleford for his editorial assistance; In Chung for data analyses; and Cheryl McClure for word-processing assis-tance. Each of us owes a great deal to special colleagues whose ideas shared in discussions over the years helped shape many of the ideas appearing in this book: Ellen acknowledges the years of collaboration with and ideas of Michael Chen of Tel Aviv Univer-sity; Sharon acknowledges those of Anne DeFanti of the Rhode

Island Department of Education and Jan Phlegar of the Regional Laboratory for Educational Improvement in the Northeast and the Islands. Ellen also thanks Samuel Bacharach for his initial encouragement and ongoing support. Sharon recognizes the ideas and support she has received from the Coalition of Essential Schools at Brown University while she was studying the principal at a Coalition School. We also appreciate input from our colleagues in the Department of Educational Leadership at Vanderbilt. Finally, we thank all the principals, superintendents, and teachers who have let us into their schools, their lives, and their minds, reinforcing our knowledge that principals-in-charge of dynamic schools *do* exist.

About the Authors

Ellen B. Goldring is Associate Professor of Education in the Department of Educational Leadership at Peabody College of Vanderbilt University where she teaches courses in organizational theory and quantitative methods. Her research interests include examining the impact of changing forces, both internal and external to the school, on the nature of principals' work. In a broad international perspective, she studies the link between parental involvement and public schools of choice. Specifically, her work focuses on the way increased parental involvement impacts the principal and how principals and parents interact. Following this line, she is looking at principals who work in schools that have undergone major change efforts. She has published articles in such journals as *Educational Administration Quarterly, Educational Policy,* and *Urban Education.*

Goldring received her doctorate from the University of Chicago. She has teaching experience at the elementary and junior high level and has been an evaluator for the Chicago Board of Education in the Department of Educational Research and Evaluation. In this position she evaluated innovative programs such as Paideia Schools. Before coming to Vanderbilt, she was on the faculty at Tel

Aviv University where she was Chair of the Program in Educational Administration and Organization.

Sharon F. Rallis is Associate Professor of Education in the Department of Educational Leadership at Peabody College of Vanderbilt University where she teaches courses in inquiry, administrative problem solving, and qualitative methods. Her research interests focus on alternative images of leadership in education and on practitioners' use of the products of inquiry. In the past, she has studied the conditions that support change efforts. Currently, she is exploring the role of school boards in school improvement. Interested in the development of board members, she is working to design and test training experiences. She is also looking at leaders' use of evaluation information. She has published in *Phi Delta Kappan, Evaluation Practice*, and the *National Society for the Study of Education Yearbook.*

Rallis received her doctorate from Harvard University. She has been a school principal and a classroom teacher at all levels, K-12. She has also served as a member of a local school board where she collaborated to design a new school. Before coming to Vanderbilt, she was a Senior Research Associate in a university center for evaluation and research, where she worked with teachers, principals, and superintendents in schools developing and evaluating various educational programs.

Principals-in-Charge

Embracing New Forces

*What are the forces that are changing the nature of the princi-
palship? Where are they coming from? Are they new and different
from the forces that shaped the schools of yesterday? How are they
affecting schools? Lee's thoughts about being a principal in this era
provide some insight into these forces.*

Lee had a few minutes to gobble a sandwich before heading off to
the school board meeting. Having been principal of Vibrant Springs
School for 5 years, Lee was fairly confident that the board would
support the school's proposal for schedule changes and student
advisory periods. Members of the school planning council would
be with Lee at the meeting. Although the plan had been a product
of this council (which consisted of teachers, parents, and community members), the council had asked that the principal present it
to the board to indicate its legitimacy and its feasibility. The
members were aware, as was Lee, that the board was not ready to
grant total authority to empowered teachers or parents.

As principal of a school that had chosen to make changes in its
structures and processes, in roles and relationships, Lee had already
had a busy day. A meeting with a lawyer of a handicap advocacy
group had started the day. The group was representing students
in a districtwide class action suit to obtain additional services. Lee

had arranged this meeting to discuss alternative solutions generated by the teacher alternative support (TAS) teams. These teams were the outgrowth of various federal and state projects to encourage collaborative problem solving by teachers in schools.

Next, Lee met with the student advisory council, a subsidiary of the school planning council. These students, identified by the total council, represented the leadership of a range of student factions throughout the school: the athletes, the scholars, the musicians, and the auto shop group, to name a few. Lee chuckled at the memory of the orchestra head sitting next to the head of the Rappie group, and the lead cheerleader across from the rep of the Young Mothers' group. The focus for the semester has been alternative outcome assessment. Students, as well as parents, are responding to the national call for determining ways to assess learning that would be responsive to the diverse abilities and skills that students bring with them to school. Lee was pleased with the students' reaction to Julio and Dan-Ling's proposal to include some native language questions on the composition test. "This was a start, at least," thought Lee. The group agreed to bring the idea to the TAS team to garner teacher support before taking any such proposal to the school advisory council.

The students had also raised another issue for future discussion—encouraging teachers to use alternative technology in their classrooms. The rep from Junior Achievement pointed out that business and industry scoff at the lecture method for training. The young man reported that interactive videodiscs and simulations were commonly used. He suggested that the students work with the school council to find support for teacher training in the use of these new materials. Lee had been impressed with his plea for technology in the classroom—schools need to prepare students to be competitive in industry. When Lee reminded the group that resources were limited in public schools, another student suggested that they invite several business leaders to inform faculty and students about new training technology.

Coincidentally, Lee was scheduled to have lunch that day with the town's Rotary Club. At lunch, the principal had introduced the idea to a local corporate executive. Although they did explore potential connections for training teachers in technology methodology, Lee knew their discussion was only a first step. Lee was equally cautious in predicting success for the other project raised with the Rotarians: the possibility of funding a parents' room in the school, which could be staffed with interpreters and a part-time counselor. Lee was pretty sure no one had bought the idea, but he may have planted a seed.

After lunch, Lee took what has become known as the *principal's walk* through the school—a daily ritual. During the walk, Lee saw the progress on a student/teacher initiative to build a commons area for snacking and meeting. Lee also saw some graffiti scrawled across some lockers near the back entrance. Lee made a note to tell the maintenance man as well as to raise the issue of vandalism at the next advisory council meeting.

At one point in the afternoon, Lee met with Mr. and Mrs. Stubitz, whose son Mitch had been acting up in Spanish class. The vice principal (VP) for discipline had decided to suspend Mitch, and his parents were furious with the school. They had insisted on seeing the principal. "Discipline problems are never easy, no matter how often we deal with them!" thought Lee.

When classes were over for the day, Lee caught a few minutes of basketball practice, dropped in on a meeting of a team of teachers who wanted to expand the school newspaper to serve the community, and met briefly with the search committee (made up of four teachers, Lee, and a parent) for the vacant faculty position. Lee also found time to talk to the superintendent about the plan to open a child-care center in the home economics area for children of students and faculty.

"No time to do paperwork today," Lee muttered. "If tonight goes well, we will have even more of it trying to get state permission to make these changes. But the work is worthwhile, if I can see all the groups working together and not at cross-purposes."

*   *   *

We anticipate that anyone reading our description of Lee will have several questions.

- Is Lee real?
- If so, where did we meet Lee?
- Why does Lee behave this way?

Lee, although our creation, is very real to us. Lee is a composite of many principals we have met, seen, talked to, worked with, heard stories about, and surveyed. We have met Lee in small schools and in large schools, in wealthy suburbs and in poor sections of cities. We have seen Lee at work in rural and in urban schools. Lee is a minority female in one school and a white male in another, a young dynamo in one, a mature strength in another. The youngsters in Lee's school are from every kind of home with every kind of background and need.

Rich or poor, large or small, urban or rural, all the schools have one commonality—all are schools that are making changes, changes to meet the needs of their varying contexts. They are what we have noticed and labeled as *dynamic schools* because these are school organizations in which many changes are occurring simultaneously at many levels. They are not places where a single innovation is displayed as proof of superiority. Rather they are schools that are examining their quality and exploring ways to improve. Structural changes such as alternative scheduling are being attempted; processes, such as teacher hiring or problem solving, are being altered; and relationships between teachers, administrators, students, parents, and community are being developed in new images. In sum, these are dynamic schools, and Lee is their principal.

We are not attributing the changes to Lee. The contexts are far too complex, and so many forces are at work effecting these changes that we would be foolish to assume that one person could master all the forces. Still, a person with Lee's priorities, who makes the choices Lee does, who relates with people as Lee does is principal of a dynamic school. This principal recognizes and responds to the forces in the environment while also empowering others in the context to deal with the various forces. Lee facilitates the forces internally, carries the banner externally, and brings harmony between. Having, as principal, created a responsive context, Lee does not need to be constantly reactive, continually putting out fires. Truly, this principal is in charge, choosing to facilitate internally, to define externally, and to harmonize the various, often divergent, worlds within and without. Lee is not a superperson; these principals encounter roadblocks and experience failures. In fact, because principals like Lee take stands and articulate them, they often get battered. They get tired. They have limits. They take charge of their environment, however, shaping it for their schools' purposes.

Forces Behind the Emergence of Principals-in-Charge

New and complex forces are at play in the emergence of dynamic schools and the principals in charge of them. These forces, coming from both inside and outside the school, are placing totally different demands on the principal. By examining the forces that influence the principal, we can better understand Lee's behavior and why principals-in-charge evolve.

Specifically, we believe that five major forces, some internal to the school and some external, impact the principalship and that these forces are responsible for the emergence of principals-in-charge and the development of dynamic schools. These forces are listed below.

- Teachers are becoming teacher-leaders.
- Student bodies are more diverse with variant needs.
- Parents have become more vocal and action-oriented advocates.
- The social and technological contexts of schools are more complex.
- Federal and state governments are mandating restructuring activities and standards.

These forces are at work in schools. Recognizing and acknowledging that these forces exist is the first step in leading a dynamic school. Faced with numerous challenges, the principal has several options in dealing with the forces: The principal can ignore them—to the peril of the school; the principal can react to them—allowing them to drive the school; or the principal can take charge—using them to shape a dynamic school. The latter principal is one we call a principal-in-charge. This chapter examines these forces.

Teachers Are Becoming Empowered Teacher-Leaders

The most immediate force affecting the principal-in-charge may be the teachers. As a body, whether through collective bargaining or through informal or formal collaborative decision making, and as individuals who have direct contact with students in their classrooms, teachers shape the daily operations of the school. Principals-in-charge must put forth major efforts to activate and entice teachers to be motivated and committed to change efforts. Teachers are the agents of change—without them, implementation cannot take hold and change cannot occur. Teachers who believe that their contributions are recognized and that they have some say in the definition of the school norms and culture are a positive force for the school and for the principal. These teachers press for school improvement and growth.

Teacher leadership is expected to reinforce teacher motivation in contributing to school improvement. Furthermore, teacher leadership is expected to "entice teachers to stay in the profession and assure ambitious and talented young people that teaching will afford them advancement opportunities" (Hart, 1987, p. 495). Mobilizing teachers to assume leadership roles, however, is not an easy prospect. Principals-in-charge are willing and able to sustain leadership in a wide range of people and roles. These principals encourage teachers to go beyond their traditional roles and to function as counselors and managers (Shedd & Bacharach, 1991). They empower teachers to make decisions and act as they see appropriate. In response, these teachers view themselves as possessing a body of knowledge and skills they use to serve their clients: their students. They see themselves as professionals. They take credit for the school's focus and progress at the same time they acknowledge the principal's role in empowering them. Even though they do not hold formally identified leadership roles, they are leaders.

Predominantly female, this body of teacher-leaders is, in many ways, like the "Our Miss Brooks" of the 1950s television sitcom about a schoolteacher. Both are experienced, with today's teachers averaging 15 years in the classroom. Both work with, not against, the system. Both are dedicated to their students' learning. As professionals, they are committed to improving their practice in an exemplary way.

But unlike Miss Brooks, today's teachers have lives outside the classroom. They have raised families, and some have held other jobs. Many play active roles as volunteers in their communities. Their level of education is higher today, because most states require an advanced degree for permanent certification. Many graduated from college during the 1960s. Therefore, whether they participated in the protest movement or not, they had the opportunity to learn the lessons of power politics. And today, most teachers belong to collective bargaining units that afford them both power and constraints.

Because most schools are organized as bureaucratic hierarchies, teacher leadership often tends to be informal with hallway networks and teachers' room cliques. This informal leadership among teachers has socialized and sustained newcomers for years. More and more instances of formal structures empowering teachers, however, are appearing in schools. Collaborative problem-solving teams, site-based management teams, career ladder and differentiated staffing structures all offer new possibilities for teacher-leaders to emerge as a positive force toward school improvement. The principal-in-charge recognizes this force and acknowledges the many difficulties in promoting teacher leadership.

Although teacher leadership is becoming more prevalent—and is even desired by some regular classroom teachers—it reinforces role ambiguity and complicates work relationships within the school context. Teacher appointments to new leadership positions revolutionize traditional division of labor and alter the structure of authority and rewards. Overlapping and contradicting job ladders and definitions, ambiguous pay hierarchies, differential prescriptions of duties and rewards associated with different combinations of teaching and administrative assignments are introduced into the school. These new trends disrupt the traditional rules of collegiality based on unified salary schedules that provide increments only for seniority and for increasing levels of training and proficiency (Bacharach & Shedd, 1989). Mixing teaching with leadership roles changes the nature of teaching as a profession essentially homogeneous in its role definitions, demands, and expectations (Conley, 1990).

This changing situation tends to estrange the teacher-leader from former colleagues. A problematic, hierarchical distance grows between regular teachers and the new leadership core composed of teacher-leaders, teacher-supervisors, teacher-masters, and mentors (Chen & Goldring, 1992). As a result, tensions and ambiguities hover in this new organizational culture in which different teachers fulfill various hierarchical, curricular, and administrative roles (Blase, 1989).

The tensions and ambiguities are intensified for prospective teacher-leaders by the absence of any formal transition from teaching to administration and by the absence of any acceptable procedures for socialization, training, promotion, and appointment of regular teachers to leadership positions. Hart and Murphy (1990) insist that

> little attention to date has been paid to the critical need to change socialization structures and processes for teachers who expect to function in leadership roles. While studies point to the importance of socialization in all work settings and in redesigned teacher work . . . most restructure and redesign plans include no provisions for . . . the radical work-change process. (p. 245)

Given the complexity of the school context as teachers become empowered leaders, the principal's role must change. This new role is discussed in Chapter 3.

Student Bodies Are More Diverse
With Variant Needs

Another force with which the principal contends daily inside the school is the diversity of the student body and the variant and pressing needs students bring with them. This diversity carries many opportunities as well as challenges. The changing demographics of our nation are evident in our schools' student bodies, which reflect an array of colors and languages and national heritages. This multicultural cornucopia can provide a rich resource to a school, if the principal and teachers can recognize and tap into the riches. Doing so, however, can be a challenge. The school will serve as a primary opportunity for socialization, but as student diversity increases, the task becomes more difficult and the outcome more unpredictable.

Because racial issues were not solved with desegregation (Orfield & Monfort, 1988), school leaders continue dealing with inequities and tensions between black and white students. Other minority children, whether they be Native American or Hispanic-American or Asian-American or others, add to the mix, thereby increasing the potential for inequities and tensions. The principal cannot ignore the racial and cultural mix: The opportunity is to capitalize on each group's contribution to the environment; the challenge is to address the inequities and to reduce the tensions.

The mix is augmented by the new influx of immigrants. Predominantly from Southeast Asia, the Hispanic islands, Mexico and countries of Central and South America, and recently from Eastern Europe and Russia, these immigrant children bring more than their rich heritage and languages. Some of the children arrive with limited schooling, while others have had educational experiences similar to those of students in the United States. They also often come with little or no proficiency in English. To facilitate their success in their new schools, the school must provide English as a second language (ESL) instruction or limited English proficiency (LEP) classes. Depending on their background and social class, some are lacking variant experiences with their own language as well, adding the task of language development to their curriculum (see California State Department of Education, Bilingual Education Office [CSDE], 1986, for a discussion of the sociocultural contexts of language development). In both cases, the leader is challenged to bring these children into the school community without their being labeled as deficient.

But diversity in schools is not limited to cultural, racial, or ethnic diversity. The changing structural and economic characteristics of households contribute another dimension. This form of diversity brings children with more hidden needs—emotional, social, and economic needs. The following statistics provide insight into the challenges principals now face with the many sociological and psychological problems affecting today's students (Cooley, 1993):

- One of every two marriages end in divorce.
- A total of 24% of the children under 18 live with one parent (nearly 70% of these children live with the mother).
- A total of 51% of women return to work before their child reaches the age of one.
- Nearly one of every six families with related children were living in poverty in 1987.
- Nearly 16% of children are living in a stepfamily.
- Suicide is the second largest killer among individuals between the ages of 14 and 25.
- The United States leads all developed countries in number of teenagers giving birth and having abortions.
- Approximately 56 million American families indicated alcohol-related problems; child abuse was reported by 41% of families.

The assumption that children live with two biological parents, one working in the home and the other in the formal labor force is accurate in less than 33% of all families (Kirst, McLaughlin, & Massell, 1989). Children who live in single-parent families come with an emerging set of needs. Many of these families, often headed by females, suffer economic hardship. The lack of any male authority figure in the home may have behavioral consequences outside the home. The tension and stress accompanying divorce can produce children with various emotional problems. Again, children come to school daily with these problems, and numerous others not mentioned, that present a challenge to schools.

Associated with this diversity in race, ethnicity, gender, and family structure is a greater tendency toward poverty. In the past 2 decades the percent of children in America living in poverty increased from 14% to 20% (Kirst et al., 1989). These children are less likely to have access to adequate health care and nutrition than their more affluent peers. Poverty produces health problems and stress on family relationships, both of which add stress on the school.

Recognition in the mid-1970s of one of the largest groups of minorities has changed schools in yet another way. The adoption of PL 94-142 in 1976 identified the student with a disability as an integral part of the student body, introduced the concept of mainstreaming to the general school public, and made the local school responsible for serving the multiple and variant needs of all children with disabilities. Handicaps to be served range from, among others, learning disabilities to mental retardation to physical disabilities. During the first decade following the passage of the law, identification of students with disabilities in schools increased by 141.6% (U.S. Department of Education [USDE], 1988).

Mainstreaming resulted largely in pull-out services provided by resource teachers, self-contained classrooms, or both. In recent years, however, the law has been reinterpreted to support integration and inclusion of the handicapped, as seen in the implementation of least restrictive environment (LRE) or regular education initiative (REI) efforts (see, e.g., Ainscow, 1991). This movement, which places the child with a disability and services for this child in the regular classroom, has created the need for new configurations and relationships, such as coteaching, in the classroom. It also introduced new responsibilities for the classroom teacher. For example, a child with severe multiple sclerosis may require the presence of a medical aide and a computer in the classroom as well as special tutoring and a wheelchair. Additional problems with special education today include the increased academic failure of students with disabilities in regular classes, the increase in arrests of students with disabilities, and the failure of these students to find productive employment after they leave school (USDE, 1989, 1990).

Finally, the adolescents in today's student body fill schools in greater number than in the past, and they are involved in numerous activities, not all positive. Although we do not know the effect of work on teenagers and their relationships with school, many are part of the formal labor market; in 1985, more than half of all 16- to 19-year-olds worked during the year. Pregnancy, alcohol, drugs, gangs, and suicide all make up part of the adolescent culture and the schools they attend (Kirst et al., 1989).

Today's student body is a diverse mix of colors and backgrounds, and the differences are deeper than physical. We recognize that the student comes with a variety of needs. Many are poor; others are emotionally or socially deprived. Some know only their native language; others have specific learning disabilities. Some have medical needs, large or small. Repercussions of adolescent suicide are calling for a special type of leadership from principals as well (Dempsey, 1986). Whatever the need, these children are in our schools, and to some extent, society looks to the school to meet these needs. In sum, the awareness of the needs, rights, and contributions of the various groups introduces a vast set of demands and expectations on curricular, as well as extracurricular, offerings and on those who lead the school. Today's principals must expand their roles to deal with these issues.

Principals Are Interacting More With Parents

Because reform efforts, such as school-based management and schools of public choice, include a heavy parental involvement component, public school principals are being called on to be more responsive to their parent clientele (Epstein & Connors, 1992). This increased parental involvement is, in part, in response to three trends. One trend emerges from the research that maintains parental participation is an important component of the effective school (Clark, Lotto, & McCarthy, 1980). Although the research findings are mixed and seem to vary according to the social status of the parents, increased parent-school relationships appear to lead to significant educational benefits (Becker & Epstein, 1982; Hoover-Dempsey, Bassler, & Brissie, 1987). Evidence from specific programs aimed at enhancing parental involvement, such as *curriculum of the home,* has documented increased achievement among students (Henderson, 1981).

Another trend that has contributed to the view that principals should be encouraged to establish closer relationships with the parental community is the acceptance, both in theory and in practice, of the strong assertion that educational organizations are interconnected with their environments (Meyer & Rowan, 1977). The boundaries of schools are recognized as very permeable, and principals, as boundary-spanning incumbents, are in place to link the internal functioning of the school with the environment (see Thompson, 1967).

Principals' boundary-spanning tasks are crucial in large-scale educational systems where decentralization and *structural looseness* are linked with cries for community control and federally mandated parent advisory councils. For instance, Peterson (1976) notes that in Chicago, decentralization was coupled with increased parental demands and expectations. Crowson and Porter-Gehrie (1980) describe the need for the principals in a large urban city to cope with parental demands. Their study shows how principals used specific mechanisms to handle parental demands: Principals channeled parents' desires for influence toward specific functions that were under the principals' direction, principals showed flexibility and openness toward the parents' appeals, and principals worked with parents to transmit their demands to the educational system. Countless other examples exist of parent advisory councils that are central to reform efforts.

The third trend that supports increased principal-parent contact is the recent, expanding literature alleging the relative superiority of private schools compared with public schools (Coleman & Hoffer, 1986). One explanation offered for this difference is the nature of school-parent interactions in the respective sectors. In private schools, principals must respond to market forces (i.e., parental preferences and interest) because parents in private schools can withdraw their children (Cibulka, 1988). Consequently, private school principals have direct incentives to make the goals of the school congruent with those of the parental clientele. This congruent *value orientation*, or functional community, is one factor that is believed to contribute to the effectiveness of private schools (Coleman, 1987).

Private schools and public schools of choice such as magnet schools also differ from public neighborhood schools because of principals' expectations of parents. Under conditions of choice, principals can expect and demand more from parents. Because parents have chosen the school, principals can require that parents meet the school's expectations for involvement and help (Bauch, 1989).

The call that public school principals be more responsive to their parental clientele is complicated by the dual position a principal holds as both chief administrator at the building level and subordinate to central office administrators. Public school principals are required to follow district policies, but they must also respond to the volatile demands of the parents. Hence, principals are often faced with "trying to satisfy political and administrative imperatives simultaneously" (Bacharach, 1981, p. 4). Principals are in the middle and are street-level bureaucrats as they interact with parents within the context of the district hierarchical system of control.

In this new reality, the borders between schools and their communities are becoming increasingly less clear. Principals are no longer only in charge of a well-defined school organization; they must also contend with parents who have become a vocal force both in and out of the school.

The Social and Technological Contexts
of Schools Are More Complex

"The school does not exist in a void" (Cunningham, 1990, p. 12). It is highly embedded in the social context of its surrounding communities. This social context has a tremendous impact on the school and the principal. The social fabric of society reveals a tapestry of families with diverse structures, employment arrangements, racial and ethnic backgrounds, health-care needs, and support systems. These not only place new demands on schools but also place principals in a pivotal role in meeting this wider array of community needs. The social context no longer resembles white, Anglo-Saxon, rural Protestant America (Beck & Murphy, 1993).

Schools can no longer close their doors to their surrounding communities. A good example of the new demands being placed on schools as they are expected to help with the total needs of children are the coordinated-integrated services (also called wraparound services) that are connected to many schools. For instance, in Ottawa County, Michigan, schools and other social service agencies have joined together to coordinate a wide range of services for children and their families. The assistance provided includes employment counseling and housing assistance. Other integrated service programs focus on the health and nutritional needs of families, as well as linkages with community agencies (Crowson & Boyd, 1992).

These new initiatives, aimed at meeting the needs of a wide range of types of children and their families, place new and different demands on the school and the principal. The school is no longer responsible only for educating the child; it is responsible for the total well-being of the child. Principals are now involved in programs and activities beyond the school curriculum. They interact with professionals beyond classroom teachers and guidance counselors. They also work with community leaders to involve students in community work (Eberly, 1993). Principals work with parents in a variety of capacities, not only as the parents of the students in the school.

The social context of schools is also changing in relation to economic realities. Incidents of school closings owing to lack of funding and major education budget cuts are not rare. The economic crises facing school systems are mirrored in society at large as problems of the global world economy have an impact on the United States and its educational system. An interesting paradox is that school systems are singled out as both the cause of and the cure for the economic depression. The combination of blame and hope exert increasing pressures on schools.

Educators are expected to prepare young men and women for the technological reality they will face when they enter the workplace. The rapidly changing job market requires changes in the ways students are prepared. Students need to know how to interact with technology, but they must change their thinking patterns to those of independent problem solvers. The electronic classroom is just one essential aspect of meeting these demands and pressures. Other changes include teaching foreign languages, promoting interdisciplinary programs, and developing multiple-career preparation (Cromer, 1984).

Technology also has important implications for principals as leaders and managers. "The link between leadership and the work of teaching depends upon the management of one resource: information" (Rhodes, 1988). Technology should be viewed as a leadership tool. Technology can be of use to principals as they change the nature of their schools as workplaces. No longer do real barriers need to isolate people as they make decisions if technology is used.

Hence, to be part of the global economy, prepare students for careers in the future, and meet the needs of a changing family clientele, schools are being required to adapt to a new era. Principals, as leaders of these institutions, are crucial mediators between their schools and these new demands of the external context.

State and Federal Reform Mandates
Are Establishing Priorities

As the national educational reform movement enters into its second decade, emphasis is shifting to the local school: its organization and its delivery of services to the child. Murphy (1991) captures and assesses the phenomena of restructured schools that focus inward. Districts choosing to restructure their schools are decentralizing, using site-based management and other tools to bring the locus of decision making closer to the point of contact between the teacher and student. But, as Murphy (1991) notes,

Freedom from district level controls and restrictions imposed by union contracts will lead to only marginal increases in local options if state and federal government agencies continue to ensnarl schools in ever-expanding webs of regulations and prescriptions. (p. 42)

Thus restructuring and reform have created a paradox for school leaders: At once, they are being urged to take matters into their own hands, while state regulations are removing control from their hands.

The state role changed in response to the education reports of the 1980s (e.g., National Commission on Excellence in Education [NCEE], 1983) that alerted the country to what became labeled a crisis in schooling. These reports decried the decline in student outcome measures (see Murphy, 1990a, for a discussion of this issue) and the reduced economic competitiveness of the United States in the world market (Underwood, 1990). In reaction, state lawmakers and governors decided they needed to take over where the local policymakers had failed. Their moves were supported by the waning federal interest in education (Underwood, 1990). Only in the areas for which specific federal laws exist (such as the education of all handicapped children through the Individuals and Disabilities Act [IDEA]) has the federal government retained some control. Rather than set policy, the U.S. Department of Education has chosen to drop its dollars, with only general restrictions and guidelines, into the states' departments of education.

The result of these two conditions, the cry of crisis and the lifting of federal influence, was a shifting of power and policy setting to the state. Claiming that districts have failed, states have moved into areas of responsibility, including curriculum and standards, that have traditionally fallen to local school boards. "State legislatures [are] acting as superschool boards, and telling the school districts and administrators how to manage the schools" (Underwood, 1990, p. 141).

Another condition, fiscal inequity across districts, has also driven control away from the local level to the state. With the aim to attain greater fiscal equity among districts, and to aid local districts with diminished capacity to afford adequate education, state funding has increased. Plans to address inequities across districts reduced aid to certain districts while substantially increasing aid to others. The increases, however, have not come without strings. Some states have attached dollars to outcomes or to specific curricular initiatives. As one example among many, the Rhode Island legislature mandated that, beginning in 1988, local school districts set aside a percentage of their state aid allocations to be spent on approved literacy initiatives. Furthermore, not all reform mandates brought any funding with them.

Increased academic content is one of the major themes running through the state-sponsored reforms. Increased graduation requirements, statewide testing aligned with curriculum, stronger attendance requirements, increases in allocated instruction time, and establishment of curriculum and materials standards are all examples of efforts in various states to fix schools. Another theme, improving the teacher force, reveals states' adopting strategies such as stiffer certification requirements, career ladders, and performance-based evaluation, among others. Finally, states have mandated programs to address specific populations and their needs, such as at-risk youth, the gifted, and early childhood education (Firestone, Fuhrman, & Kirst, 1990). Many of these state-initiated programs left the details up to the local school district or school, but the first level of choice, that is, to have the program or not, had already been usurped.

The principal is pulled in opposite directions by the tension of this paradox. Yet the principal is the prime catalyst in bringing about meaningful change (English & Hunt, 1990). How do school leaders meet top-down regulations from outside their districts while still fostering an enhanced collegial on-line sense of initiative and control within their schools? The principal must be in charge to meet this challenge.

Summary

In this chapter, we described the new and complex forces that are imposing entirely different demands on the principalship.

Ignoring or resisting these forces to maintain the status quo signals failure for our schools. In response to these changing organizational contexts, principals, if their schools are to be active and positively changing schools, must take on new roles and revise their leadership styles. As leaders of these new types of schools, they must be principals-in-charge. We are calling these changed schools *dynamic schools.* In the next chapter, we describe the type of school that is emerging in response to these forces and the types of schools where principals-in-charge work.

The Dynamic School

How are schools responding to the forces pressing on them today? Some schools are being driven by the forces, but others, like Lee's school, are involved in many changes, proactively searching for improvement. What kind of school does a principal like Lee work in? What is a dynamic school?

The sun was breaking through the morning clouds as Lee parked in the principal's spot at Vibrant Springs. Lee was returning after being gone a week on an accreditation team visit to a school in another part of the state. "That school did not appear to have been touched by reform. How could they be meeting all the needs of kids today with their business-as-usual attitude? Vibrant Springs is different—we have so much going on here!" Lee began to think about reasons for the positive feelings about the school and felt a deep sense of pride in the school.

"We are making choices to restructure. And we have a lot to choose from. We've just been selected as one of the Governor's Schools, so that means new programs and resources. I think I scheduled a preplanning session for the next release day. And we are in our second year of that IBM computer support program— what a difference that has made! Kids whom I never envisioned on a computer are comfortable on them now. Anne at the state department of education said that we have one of the most active teacher assistance teams. The regional lab is coming down to do further training in that assessment project. And the parents' group is sponsoring another peer counseling program. If I think some more, I'm sure I'll come up with other programs. Sometimes I can barely keep them straight, but they all have a place.

"Do we have too much going on? Sometimes I wonder, but I think not. Each program belongs to somebody or meets a specific need. The programs are what give us options, choices. They help create resources. They contribute to the atmosphere here I value so much—that learning is exciting, that there is more than one way to do something."

Lee thought about what made the school work so well with its myriad programs. Clearly, the teachers played an important role. "The teachers here are professionals. They don't just come to work, teach, and go home—they take responsibility for making this a place where kids can really learn. Sure, we still have a few deadbeats, but they are a minority. Most are pressing for improvement as much as, if not more than, I am. They want to make decisions that will affect the school. They give so much of their time, their knowledge, their energy. I could not be the principal I want to be without their willingness to be a part of the whole school process."

Then, Lee watched a parent walk into the building. "Parents, too—they make a difference at Vibrant Springs. They let me know when I am on track, and the minute I get off, they let me know that, too! I can count on them to fight for resources when they are behind the idea."

Lee thought about resources. Vibrant Springs seemed to be resource-rich compared with the school Lee had visited that week. "But our community is not any wealthier. People at Vibrant Springs just seem to find the resources. Maybe we create them—resources seem to beget more! All the programs we are involved in, all the parents' activities, and all the time and energy people are willing to spend. Of course, we always need more, but someone always finds a way.

"And I don't feel we're alone. That other school seemed so isolated from the rest of the world. Vibrant Springs seems to be part of the world. Certainly, we are part of the community we live in.

"I suppose I should take a little credit myself," Lee thought while walking into the school. "After all, I do listen and support.

I let people know where I stand; I communicate. It's important to me to help others do their jobs well—to involve those who need to be involved.

"I know the world is changing, and that schools must change too. But I believe that schools have choices about what they want to become. I don't feel driven or bewildered. I feel that together we can decide and make positive choices to improve our schools. Yes, I feel pretty good about this school—and about myself as principal."

*   *   *

Lee's thoughts reveal a principal who is in charge of change, who recognizes that schools need to be restructured, consciously and with direction, to meet the needs and demands of a changing society. But not all schools are dealing with change in the positive way that Lee's school has chosen. Lee's school is what we have called a dynamic school. This chapter defines the dynamic school and describes what the insides of these schools look like.

Throughout the past decade numerous commissions and studies have aimed to reform the state of education. What has become known as the *reform movement* has been the center of educational thought and debate. Conservative organizational perspectives largely dominate the emphasis on reform implementation (Clark, Lotto, & Astito, 1984). Generally, a bureaucratic view of schools as organizations is assumed. Principals are viewed as goal-directed individuals who consider and evaluate school problems, actively seeking solutions and implementing change to achieve specific goals (Leithwood & Montgomery, 1982). Hence principals should be primarily concerned with productivity and, consequently, change structures and technology to increase productivity (Bolman & Deal, 1984). In their search for increased productivity, principals would implement reform efforts as a way to respond to social and political pressures. According to this view, one may expect that principals with the most school problems would be the most likely to adopt change efforts.

As we know, however, this conservative view does not always represent the reality of schools; principals are not always rational and goal directed. Great variability exists in the extent to which schools and principals implement change and respond to reform efforts. Even mandated changes are not uniformly implemented. In fact, as the reform movement gains momentum, criticisms are mounting that these reform efforts seem to have little impact on changes in schools (Ginsberg & Wimpelberg, 1987).

Dynamic schools, however, are those that *are* actively involved in change efforts that make a difference. These are schools, such as Lee's school, that are responding to the several forces that are having an impact on them and proactively searching for improvement. Dynamic schools vary in the number of changes that they adopt and in their selection of these changes, but they take on complex, difficult changes because the internal mechanisms to sustain change efforts are either already in place or are being simultaneously developed. At this juncture, the principal becomes crucial. The dynamic school principal coordinates, motivates, and activates the total school community to implement and sustain change in an ongoing search for growth and improvement.

What Is a Dynamic School?

Dynamic schools are schools that take charge of change. Rather than reacting to and being driven by the forces impacting schools today, or pretending such forces do not exist, the dynamic school seizes them as opportunities to improve itself. Thus numerous changes occur in dynamic schools. These schools constantly learn and grow with an aim toward improving. They respond; they choose innovation and activities to address the needs they see and feel. The environments are active, contributing and receiving, as opposed to static and rejecting. Lee is the principal of such a school. Lee works in a school that is adopting new changes, reviewing old changes, and engaging in ongoing processes of self-evaluation.

How do we know that dynamic schools really exist? First, studies that have examined the processes of change in schools in the past decades (see, e.g., Berman & McLaughlin, 1975; Huberman & Miles, 1984) repeatedly found that substantial change efforts that addressed multiple problems were more likely to succeed and survive than were small-scale, easily trivialized innovations. The Rand Change Agent Study (Berman & McLaughlin, 1978) links school culture with school improvement outcomes. More recently, McLaughlin (1987) suggests that cultural characteristics of schools, such as teacher commitment, motivation, and will, are locally defined and driven. In other words, some schools seem to demonstrate a culture of change. Thus research documents the presence of schools where numerous changes are employed with an aim toward improving the total environment of the school.

In addition, actual examples supporting the concept of dynamic schools appear in the literature of the past decade. Lightfoot (1983), in *The Good High School,* portrays several schools that qualify as dynamic schools. She paints Brookline High School as a school that has chosen to deal with diversity and changing times as a resource and strength, rather than a weakness. She presents George Washington Carver High School as a school that has discovered the strength and resources of the community as it changes its mission to prepare its students for the work world outside Carver. Her picture of John F. Kennedy High School provides an image of how a huge (5,300 students) and diverse population can become a pluralistic community. Each of Lightfoot's schools embraces change and actively works toward improvement.

Other researchers also offer glimpses of schools where a variety of change processes are in place. Louis and Miles (1990), in their recent book on improving urban high schools, provide case studies of schools involved in implementing change. The case studies of those schools successfully moving toward improvement provide additional portraits of dynamic schools.

One such school, Agassiz High School, initially assembled "all sorts of improvement activities: the improvement program components and activities would gradually grow, and fit together in a loose but relatively integrated way" (Louis & Miles, 1990, p. 66). The variety of the change processes implemented in this school included coordinated social services, weekly staff meetings to discuss at-risk students, service delivery within the school by external agencies, ROTC, and cluster programs by grade level.

Horace's School (Sizer, 1992) offers a prototype of a dynamic school. Horace, a fictional high school teacher, chairs a committee charged by the school board to review the school's purposes and practices and to recommend a new design. In Sizer's (1992) book, the readers join the committee (composed of teachers, parents, students, a school committee member, and a visitor from the university) and learn of the school's multiple needs and hear the committee members create multiple approaches to address these needs. Although both the characters and the school are Sizer's creations, all aspects of the situation and the process are drawn from Sizer's very real experiences with schools undergoing multiple changes as a part of the Coalition of Essential Schools (the ideas of the coalition are set forth in Sizer, 1984).

Goodlad (1984) paints a picture of improved schools in *A Place Called School*. In these improved schools, multiple changes place more responsibility on the school community for making those decisions that affect the school. These self-directed schools need principals who can lead and manage in unique ways to reach solutions to problems.

The large sample of schools from the *High School and Beyond* study (USDE, 1984) helped us define a dynamic school as well. In the *High School and Beyond* survey, public secondary school principals reported changes that have occurred in their schools. Their responses are summarized in Table 2.1. This table reveals some interesting points. The majority of the changes relate to students, whereas only three relate directly to teacher work conditions and rewards. The most popular changes include increasing graduation requirements, developing new student conduct codes, and grouping students by academic ability. Longer school days and years, changes directed both at teachers and students, are implemented in relatively few of the schools (24% and 15%, respectively). The frequency of teacher-related changes indicates that only one was adopted by the majority of principals: establishing teacher performance evaluation, 54%. The other teacher-related changes are implemented by less than 13% of the principals. On the average, 39% of the 354 schools adopted each student-related new practice, whereas 19% implemented teacher-related changes.

Table 2.1 Percent of Principals Reporting Changes in School Practices (*N* = 354)

School Practice	Percent Who Responded Yes
Student Based	
Increased graduation requirements	77.6
Established new student conduct code	77.0
Grouped students by academic need	51.0
Increased homework	42.4
Instituted competency tests for graduation	45.4
Created major curriculum change	26.6
Instituted longer school day	24.1
Changed background of students	21.1
Instituted longer school year	15.5
Developed new desegregation plan	8.9
Teacher Based	
Established teacher performance evaluation	54.0
Established teacher career ladder	12.2
Established teacher financial incentives	6.6

SOURCE: Based on principals' responses to the *High School and Beyond* survey (USDE, 1984). Adapted from Chen and Goldring (1990).

Based on this survey and this list of changes, we may conclude that secondary school principals are not implementing an abundance of changes, especially as far as teachers are concerned. We continued to look at this list of changes, however, and asked ourselves a number of questions. Are principals who implement one change more likely to adopt other changes as well? Or are principals and their school systems choosing distinct, single changes rather than some combination of changes? Furthermore, we asked, who are the 47 principals (12%) who reported that they have adopted teacher career ladders? Did they choose that particular change only in isolation? These and similar questions led us to the notion of dynamic schools.[1]

To answer these types of questions we looked at the relationships, or intercorrelations, among the different changes (Table 2.2). The large number of significant correlations indicates that schools that have made one change are very likely to implement other changes. For example, the large number of significant relationships between adopting career ladders and other changes suggests that although the implementation of this change is rather infrequent (12%) whenever it is adopted it is combined with multiple change practices. This, then, is a practice achieved in a dynamic school; a school where many other changes are already in place. Similarly, principals reporting that they initiated a major curriculum change are also adopting numerous other changes, such as increased graduation standards, student grouping for instruction, increased homework, a longer school day, and a desegregation plan.

Hence an empirical definition of a dynamic school is a school that is adopting a variety of changes in search of and in response to its many communities. Throughout this book, we refer to this empirical definition as we present data from the survey of principals reported in *High School and Beyond* (USDE, 1984) that illustrate the actions of principals in dynamic schools compared with the actions of principals in schools that are much more static and traditional in their orientations. Throughout this volume you will meet principals and teachers in dynamic schools.

What Do Dynamic Schools Look Like?

The notion that internal school mechanisms support conditions for change explains what we would expect to see inside the dynamic school. The literature on change suggests that schools as organizations must have the necessary institutional arrangements and resources to support the implementation of change (Fullan, 1982). Therefore, the emergence of dynamic schools and the differential rate of the implementation of change often result from internal school processes. In dynamic schools, we see specific internal school processes. In analyzing the data from interviews,

Table 2.2 Correlations Between Changes in School Practices (N = 340)

School Practice	1	2	3	4	5	6	7	8	9	10	11	12	13
Student Based													
1. Increased graduation	1.00												
2. Student conduct code	0.06	1.00											
3. Student grouping	0.15*	0.19*	1.00										
4. Increased homework	0.18*	0.14*	0.21*	1.00									
5. Competency testing	0.09	0.11*	0.22*	0.16*	1.00								
6. Curriculum change	0.10*	0.05	0.19*	0.16*	0.21*	1.00							
7. Longer school day	0.16*	0.02	0.08	0.09	0.04	0.07	1.00						
8. Student backgrounds	0.03	0.09	0.15*	0.21*	0.18*	0.11*	0.12*	1.00					
9. Longer school year	0.16*	0.04	0.13*	0.14*	0.18*	0.11	0.46*	0.19*	1.00				
10. Desegregation plan	0.00	0.08	0.05	0.08	0.09	0.23*	0.08	0.15*	0.04	1.00			
Teacher Based													
11. Teacher evaluation	0.08	0.10*	0.07	-0.03	0.07	0.06	0.03	0.05	0.10*	0.13*	1.00		
12. Teacher career ladders	0.18*	0.03	0.13*	0.05	0.21*	0.17	0.19*	0.09	0.24*	0.00	0.16*	1.00	
13. Teacher financial incentive	0.05	0.02	0.07	0.00	0.11*	0.00	0.00	0.05	0.17*	0.00	0.13*	0.39*	1.00

*$p < .05$.

surveys, and questionnaires collected across all the schools we discuss in this volume, we noticed that dynamic schools exhibit four common characteristics: (1) supportive internal leadership, (2) teacher press for improvement (Chen & Goldring, 1990), (3) adequate resources, and (4) availability of programmatic and curricular options (see Rallis & Phleger, 1990, for the initial analyses that identified these characteristics).

Examples exist of the conditions that are present in dynamic schools. A comprehensive evaluation of a statewide, building-based change effort—the classroom alternative process (CAP) (Rallis, 1989)—gives us a view into a number of dynamic schools that fostered changes. In these schools, not only was the specific innovation working but numerous other innovations were also evident. The first condition, supportive internal leadership, was evident in building principals who facilitated the innovation by manipulating resources or options to empower those who were to operate the new program. For example, some offered comp time for those classroom teachers serving on teacher assistance teams meeting before or after school. Others procured stipends for team members. Still others found coverage for team members' classes during meetings. In addition, some principals, such as Jim from the Hope Street School, provided extra support by preparing folders for team members on each referral before the team meeting. Eileen, from Tipton Elementary, worked to see that rules were relaxed to allow for alternatives that teachers believed would provide solutions.

But these principals also encouraged atmospheres that welcomed a variety of initiatives, so several different programs were in the process of unfolding in each setting. In fact, in some of the most active schools, principals had trouble distinguishing between the different programs. One principal admitted that he was not sure how each child had gained entrance into a special reading program: "Some are referred by CAP, some are Chapter 1, some are from our slow-learner group. I think the program grew out of the commissioners' literacy initiative—I encouraged a couple of our teachers to write up a grant for some of that money, but it has grown."

Our data also showed that every one of these principals had a strong positive relationship with his or her superintendent. In all cases in which teams were thriving, the principal communicated regularly with the superintendent. Thus the superintendent was aware of the activities associated with the innovation and was, in general, supportive of the innovation. In many cases, the principal was able to facilitate team operations and/or implement team decisions because the superintendent was able to free up resources.

The second condition, teacher press for improvement, was apparent among teachers directly involved in the innovation as well as throughout the faculty. These teachers considered themselves knowledgeable and skilled; they saw themselves as professionals. "I know my students better than anyone—and I know my subject—so I am the right person to meet their needs. All I need is support to try different approaches," one teacher responded when asked why she valued CAP. Positive collegial relationships were the norm in these schools rather than the exception, so teachers collaborated to meet students' needs. "Working together on teams seems the natural way to generate solutions. The team helps me remember approaches that once worked, but I have forgotten," reported a CAP team member. The teachers in these buildings expressed high levels of self-confidence and were willing to do whatever it takes to make things work.

School conditions necessary for change include, among other things, supportive organizational arrangements for teachers, such as teacher-peer relationships and teacher recognition mechanisms. Past research indicates that teachers who have collegial peer relationships are more likely to develop and accept changes (Little, 1982). Teachers "need time to talk with each other about the new procedures, to solve problems together and help each other learn how to be effective" (Leighton & Shaw, 1990). Through joint interactions, teachers can exchange ideas and support one another as they engage in change. Dynamic schools provide numerous opportunities for teacher interaction to support their press for improvement.

The third condition, adequate resources (including time, money, and materials), was met for a variety of reasons. In some cases, resources for the particular innovation were available because the district had included a financial commitment to take on the project and, in other cases, because the programs with external funding were present in the school. In nearly all cases, resources became available because people, including the principal, were willing to locate or fight for them as needed. For example, Jim told us, "Once I decided I was behind this idea, I knew that I would go to the top to get what these teams needed." We also noted that most of the supportive principals started with, or found a way to build, strong relationships with their superintendents so they could be sure of backing from the central office.

Finally, programmatic options or alternatives and general support services took many forms. Curricular alternatives already may have been available or a variety of externally funded programs may have been in operation. Federal or state initiatives may have been offering additional choices. In some schools, the number of programs had multiplied to the point at which it was difficult to define what was part of one program and what was separate from it. Although many of the options originally may have come from outside the school (e.g., from the federal government or the Regional Labs for Educational Improvement), they took hold because the general school climate accepted and nourished options. One of the principals in a CAP school commented on the activities in his school: "One reason our CAP works is that the teachers really can implement strategies the team has proposed. We have many options available—and nobody thinks it's strange when someone does something a little different."

Descriptions in the literature portraying effective schools further elaborate our picture of dynamic schools by revealing internal processes that support change. Lightfoot (1983) introduces Carver's principal, who can "track down resources and broaden horizons" (p. 42) as he builds bridges by networking with community groups and leaders to establish programs that will link students with the working world. Kennedy's principal fosters participation and collaboration. We see him as "down in the trenches inspiring, cajoling, and encouraging people to 'do their best and give their most' " (p. 68). He also serves as a buffer, protecting his faculty members so that they have the freedom to do their best. In Brookline High

School, Lightfoot (1983) allows us to witness the town meeting designed to change patterns of power and decision making in the school. We also see the operation of houses as partial communities and the school within a school that "emerges as a real community that embraces the lives of its inhabitants" (Lightfoot, 1983, p. 186).

Louis and Miles (1990) talk about a close, cohesive internal network when describing the relationships among staff in those high schools that successfully implement change. In *Horace's School* (Sizer, 1992), teachers come to press for the changes and to seek support from a variety of sources. Finally, Goodlad (1984) emphasizes the need for a skilled principal who can secure a working consensus in the search for solutions. In all these examples, the focus is on the creation of options within the learning environment.

Summary

Lee works in a dynamic school, a school engaged in numerous changes as it works toward improvement. Lee's school can sustain these changes and the dynamic work environment because the organization relies on and develops internal processes that support change.

In this chapter we described the type of school in which Lee works as a dynamic school. Dynamic schools are emerging in light of the forces that are having an impact on schools today. Dynamic schools choose to engage in numerous change efforts to meet the multiple demands of education. The internal processes in dynamic schools are different from those in traditional schools, and hence they require a different type of principal, a principal-in-charge. In the next chapter we look at our principal-in-charge, Lee, in one of the new roles: the facilitator.

Note

1. The following analysis is based on the intercorrelations and factor analysis of this list of changes, corresponding to question P40 from the *High School and Beyond* survey. The factor analysis indicated that all of the changes constitute one factor. The positive correlations of each item with other items in the list indicates that together these changes measure the tempo of the introduction of changes for each school. The single-factor structure indicates that the tendency to adopt new practices is an unidimensional tendency. The factor weights of each item and the correlations lead to the review of the interrelationships between different types of changes. The technical details of the factor analysis are available from the authors.

3

The Facilitator

Enabling Internal Leadership

What do principals-in-charge do inside their buildings day by day? In this chapter we take a look at Lee, the facilitator. Lee's role inside the school is a leader of other adults. The principal is in charge, but many of the adults are also knowledgeable, creative professionals who can be leaders in their own right. Lee's role, then, becomes one of motivating, enabling, coordinating, and legitimizing the work of teacher-leaders within the school.

Lee had invited Walt, chair of the school planning council, to share lunchtime in the principal's office so they could discuss the group's progress. Lee had created the planning council to do more than just advise the principal; Lee saw it as being directly involved in making decisions about new directions for the school. The superintendent had agreed to give this team decision-making authority in areas like scheduling, curriculum, testing, and grades—in nearly all issues affecting instruction. To this point, Lee felt quite good about the council, which included 10 teachers and two parents, and it appeared that the council members were beginning to believe that their role was not just symbolic and that their work would shape the school's future. Still, Lee would feel more confident if Walt agreed that the group really was feeling empowered.

After both were settled, Lee asked, "So, what do you think? Are these real priorities for the teachers?"

"I guess so," answered Walt. "I mean, they must be, if most of the group is willing to go against you!"

"Now what does that mean?" Lee wondered aloud.

"Well, I figure you think that dealing with outcome assessment should be the top priority," Walt responded. "Everybody knows that's your pet theme this year—you know, you joined that national consortium on alternative assessment and were off at that workshop for a week last month—but you haven't pushed it on us yet. We were all pretty amazed yesterday when we voted to make alternative scheduling configurations our top priority—and you didn't lay down the law or try to talk us out of it."

"I guess that's because I believe new schedules are important, even necessary, too. I just thought any schedule changes should be driven by what we want the outcomes to be. But if the faculty wants to start with schedules, I respect their judgment. I didn't feel that anyone was going against me."

"I guess that's my point," Walt assured Lee. "Schedules are a real priority. They made a decision that was counter to the one you would have made, but no one felt rebellious—after all, your talking about outcomes got us to thinking that we couldn't really do anything different until we found different ways to structure time. I'd say we just felt like we had taken the first step of many. We chose which step, but you set us walking!"

They finished lunch, and Lee checked for messages received through electronic mail (e-mail). Because Lee recognized that schoolteachers have tight schedules but still need to connect and communicate with each other, the principal had made sure that everyone had an e-mail number and access to a networked computer. Lee saw this technology link as essential in a school with diverse faculty whose various schedules often kept them separate. Lee once remarked to Alma, the principal's secretary, "Everyone knows I read my e-mail, so they can always get in touch with me, no matter how big or small the issue. Think of the time that saves you—what if you had to take all those messages, or field all those questions, or schedule all those people? It makes me feel closer to my faculty, too—and there is less room for misinterpretation because I am dealing directly with people."

Lee read two messages. One was from Linda, who thanked the principal for sending her to a math teachers' association conference. "I learned much more in 2 days there than I could have learned in a month of staff development days!" the message read. In the other message, Sam thanked Lee for agreeing to support his decision not to give grades in his process writing class: "I felt much stronger telling the parents about the idea because I knew you were behind me."

Then Lee called in Alma to make several arrangements. "Let's be sure to renew our professional memberships so that we don't lose those resources. Oh, and remind me to call the Regional Lab about that training on collaborative learning they are sponsoring with the state. I'd like some of us to go. Make an appointment for me with Bruce. We need to organize our presentation for that conference on problem solving—the one we are going to in Springfield next week."

The principal continued, "I need five subs to cover classes for the search team when it meets Thursday to discuss the vacancy in music. Wait, we'll only need three, because both Wanda and Karl have teammates who will cover their classes. I need to talk to George. As union president, he can tell me if my idea to create comp time for the teachers who serve on the TAS teams that meet before and after school is a workable one. Also, I want to ask him to talk to the Rotary Club at their next luncheon; he can articulate our concerns and needs as well, if not better than I. Oh, and last, but not least, help me think of some kind of little surprise—you know, something that symbolizes success, like those apples we gave last year—for that child-care task force. It did a great job, and I don't want it to go unnoticed."

Alma left, and Lee returned to the computer to lay out a memo to the superintendent. The memo would present the facts compiled by the TAS team that showed that ESL kids were all having problems with the basal reader. Lee planned to use these data to convince Marty, the superintendent, to ask the school board for permission to purchase foreign language trade books instead of more basal readers for next year. "With good reason," Lee argued.

"Why shouldn't these teachers decide what they need and how to spend their resources?"

Before leaving for a meeting at the central office, Lee took a moment for some self-congratulation. The school had some pretty courageous teachers who were trying new and exciting approaches to creating a more productive and positive learning environment. As their principal, Lee felt proud.

*   *   *

We see that Lee is not the only leader in the school. Instead, Lee builds an atmosphere in which the natural leadership process is allowed to flourish. Lee's school, a dynamic school, is a place where it is safe to take risks, to try new ideas; it is a place where people feel secure enough to articulate and pursue their visions of what they want to become. Lee's role is one of facilitating; that is, Lee motivates, coordinates, and legitimizes the work of the teachers by taking a stand and then by manipulating time, space, resources, and personnel to enable them to join in moving toward that position. Lee does not empower; rather, Lee works to establish an atmosphere in which the teachers empower themselves to press for improvement and growth.

The task before Lee may appear overwhelming: Lee is not a superhero who can be all things to all people. Instead, Lee's strength lies in recognizing that leadership is not a commodity to be purchased or a skill to be exercised by either the principal or the teachers. Rather leadership in a dynamic school is a process of collective decision making (Rallis, 1990). Establishing the atmosphere for the effective functioning of this process is not easy, but neither was work of the white knight principal with its unidirectional, top-down flow of authority that placed all the power and responsibility in the principal's hands (see Bridges, 1977). In sum, we recognize that Lee's task to achieve shared leadership is a massive and challenging one, but we see it as reasonable and realistic.

Changing Teacher Roles:
Changing the Workplace

A sense of belonging is essential in dynamic schools where teachers' role ambiguity increases as new rules and structures place different demands and rewards on teachers. The task for principals in these schools is more complex, then, because the principals are no longer dealing with a homogeneous faculty with a single role definition and a single set of performance expectations. In dynamic schools, we see teachers in at least three levels of leadership: existing leaders, potential leaders, and followers.

First, there are those teachers who are already empowered or are ready to take on leadership roles. The principal-in-charge recognizes these teachers and enables them to be the teacher-leaders they can and want to be. Also, we see teachers who are capable of assuming leadership roles, but who may not see this potential. In these cases, the principal-in-charge motivates and encourages, showing them that teacher leadership is possible. As both of these groups take on new roles, they will need the principal's continuing support to sustain them in these roles. Finally, a faculty includes those teachers who have chosen not to assume any leadership role outside their own classroom. These teachers are important because they contribute to the essential work of the school. The principal-in-charge must respect the choice these teachers have made and must strive to see that their contributions are valued.

The coexistence of these various levels of involvement increases the likelihood for tension across groups and for resistance to change by some faculty. Facilitation and coordination are primary tasks of the principal-in-charge because this principal recognizes that the faculty's heterogeneity is a strength rather than a source of problems. Tapping this strength to encourage change in the workplace requires a principal with a full range of enabling and facilitating skills.

Enabling and facilitating teacher leadership does not mean that no one is in charge; rather the principal is in charge. To create teachers who are professional partners in the decision-making and implementation processes of the school, the principal uses specific practices to motivate and engage teachers and provides opportunities that teachers regard as rewarding. These activities lead to a sense of efficacy and accomplishment, thus stimulating an ongoing desire of teachers to continue involvement as teacher-leaders. Principals-in-charge provide opportunities that empower those teachers who wish to expand their traditional roles.

What Is Empowerment?

Facilitating the leadership of others or promoting empowerment in an organization is a complex task. Initially, it requires a focus on processes that provide opportunities for enabling internal leadership to emerge, instead of a focus on the outcomes of these processes (Michael, Short, & Greer, 1991). The role of the principal-in-charge is to "balance efforts to empower others with maintenance of a leadership presence" (Prestine, 1991). The principal draws the members of the school organization together to build a culture within which they define and pursue their mutual goals (Rallis, 1990).

Although the term *empowerment* is widely used in the restructuring rhetoric, its meanings are not always clear. When we speak about the principal-in-charge as facilitating, empowering, and enabling teacher leadership, we imply that the processes of empowerment are motivational, aimed at "creating conditions for heightening motivation for task accomplishment through the development of a strong sense of personal efficacy" (Conger & Kanungo, 1988, p. 474). Following this definition, the principal's role in facilitating leadership is to structure and provide empowering experiences for teachers in schools. Simply creating opportunities for shared decision making is not enough. Teachers must first feel empowered enough to participate in the processes and be dedicated to the new role (Taylor, 1991).

Empowerment emerges as a result of raising teachers' status, knowledge, and participation (Maeroff, 1988). In terms of status, "there will be no empowerment while teachers feel small and insignificant because they are doing a job that they think is not adequately appreciated by those outside the schools" (Maeroff, 1988, p. 474). Status can be gained through autonomy and recognition. Knowledge is enhanced when teachers are partners in defining their needs and setting agendas and are given opportunities to participate in these activities. Participation increases both knowledge and status. Teacher participation results in empowerment as teachers have a sense of control over their workplace. Participation provides teachers with "the power to exercise one's craft with quiet confidence and to help shape the way the job is done" (Maeroff, 1988, p. 475).

Empirical research supports the importance of the principal in promoting teacher leadership in schools. In a recent study in a Midwestern metropolitan school district, the extent to which teachers are willing to participate in school decision making is influenced primarily by their relationships with their principals (Smylie, 1992). These findings, supported by other research, suggest that teachers are willing to broaden their roles when they work with principals who are collaborative, open, supportive and facilitative (Johnson, 1989; Malen & Ogawa, 1988).

What Do Principals Do to Facilitate Teacher Leadership?

How does a principal-in-charge establish an atmosphere in which leadership flourishes, in which people can realize their visions? Reports about schools that are engaging teachers in empowering experiences and facilitating teacher leadership roles, as well as our own data sets, indicate that principals seem to emphasize five practices to raise teachers' status, knowledge, and participation (Goodman, 1987; Kretovics, Farber, & Armaline, 1991; Leithwood & Jantzi, 1990; Sickler, 1988):

1. motivating teachers through establishing a problem-solving climate, consensus building, and goal setting;
2. incorporating participatory decision-making mechanisms;
3. establishing opportunities for collegial peer contacts and communication;

4. providing recognition and rewards; and
5. obtaining the necessary resources and technical support to sustain all empowering processes.

Motivating Teachers for Involvement

A crucial task for principals in facilitating teacher leadership falls in the area of motivation. Leithwood and Steinbach (in press) found that highly effective principals actually worked with groups of teachers to promote motivation. They focus their group work on three issues: (a) developing better solutions to problems, (b) stimulating commitment to defensible goals, and (c) promoting long-term problem-solving skills.

This ability to motivate delineates a skill of our principals in the case studies. The interviews and observations indicate that the opportunity to connect with colleagues is often seen by empowered teachers as rewarding. The principals in our case studies often motivated their teachers by creating such collaboration experiences.

Another reward is the opportunity to connect outside the school with community or professional leaders, as indicated in the case studies. Ken, principal of Midway High School, a coalition school, provides connection opportunities as a motivating experience by earmarking some of the foundation money for substitutes and registration fees so that special teachers are able to attend conferences or relevant workshops or visit nearby schools as a reward. Marsha of the Littleton K-8, a CAP school, often chooses to send an appropriate teacher to speak in her place at some event to which she was invited. "Most of the time, one of my teachers can deliver the message better than I could—and it gets them out of the routine. I think it makes them feel good."

By creating opportunities for teachers to engage in rewarding experiences, principals-in-charge motivate teachers to be active partners in school processes and improvement efforts.

Providing Opportunities for
Authentic Participation

The linchpin of facilitating teacher leadership seems to be in developing authentic participation in decision-making forums. Empowered teachers control decisions through formal and informal roles in school governance forums (Conley, 1988). These decision-making teams are often referred to as school-based management or school improvement councils. For instance, in the Kentucky Education Reform Act of 1990, which mandated school-based decision making, teachers make up half of the council members. These councils are to have decision-making authority over such areas as the school budget, professional development, and school improvement plans (Steffy, 1990). Hallinger and Richardson (1988) identify four models of shared decision making in schools that lead to different levels of empowerment. These models are principals' advisory councils, instructional support teams, school improvement teams, and lead teacher committees.

Empowered teachers make decisions in formal school governing bodies or in informal collegial groups. Whatever the setting, empowered teachers, "the people practicing their profession, decide what is to be done and how it is to be done within the constraints imposed by the larger goals of the organization" (Carnegie Task Force, 1986, p. 39). The principal and teachers embrace the opportunity to shape school practice by recognizing, affirming, and using the collective expertise of the faculty (Rallis, 1990).

We stress the importance of the principal's commitment to authentic participation. Prestine (1991), in her case studies of four Illinois schools that are members of the Coalition of Essential Schools, indicates that lack of trust by teachers poses a severe problem in shared decision making. For instance, when principals in these schools controlled the agenda and problem identification of the shared decision-making committees, the degree of teacher participation decreased. Furthermore, when principals were not committed *themselves* to the process (realizing that shared decision making is often time-consuming, frustrating, and slow), the process was ineffective. This study indicates another important finding: One of the principal's tasks is to help facilitate teachers in their new decision-making roles and not just assume that getting a group of professionals together will result in well-conceived decisions. Training in communication, team building, and conflict resolution prove essential. Sickler (1988), reporting about the empowering process of teachers in a suburban Los Angeles school district, suggests that in addition to principal support and training for participative mechanisms a critical mass of teachers must be willing to take part in these processes in a school for participation to have an impact.

The data from the three case study projects and interviews with principals in these projects further elaborate what principals-in-charge do to facilitate teacher participation in decision making. Because the school is full of potential leaders, the principals who wished to build a dynamic school created arenas for teacher decision making. They identified and established many opportunities for these arenas: curriculum teams, instructional alternative teams, search committees for the hiring of new teachers, and budget allocation advisory committees, to name a few. These opportunities for shared decision making were perceived as real; teachers functioning in these groups believed their voices were heard, not overruled. Teachers in these groups made decisions themselves, not merely advised another who would make the decisions. The principals-in-charge from these case studies reported that they worked at ensuring that these shared decision-making opportunities were meaningful.

Consensus building represents one skill that some principals used. Because faculties are diverse and because expecting some teachers to make real decisions that will drive the operation of the school increases the tension of role ambiguity, the principals-in-charge that we observed and spoke with realized the need to work at building consensus. Although no leader can expect consensus all the time, a shared set of values and beliefs—an accepted mission—is necessary for the school to move forward. Thus goal setting is seen as a part of the consensus-building skill. Once the faculty has set priorities and agreed on a common direction, individuals are free to express themselves within these accepted boundaries. Ken, Eileen, and Larry, three principals from the case studies, illustrate this skill in practice.

Teachers on the planning team at Midway High School, a coalition school, report that Ken, their principal, builds consensus as he works with them:

> He is excruciatingly democratic! He knows he could make a decision a lot faster by himself, but he also knows that sometimes the extra time is worth it.
>
> Sometimes, I feel like we sit forever seeking agreement, but then what we end up with is something completely different from what we started with, something totally new, totally ours!

Eileen of the Tipton Elementary School, a CAP school, knows the importance of some level of consensus for her school's problem-solving team:

> I may be the principal, and my voice is important, but I work hard to be sure that the final decision is theirs, not just mine. There are two things that spell sure doom for any new idea—lack of support from my boss and lack of support from my teachers.

Larry at the Ashton Elementary School, put it this way when talking about his school's teacher assistance team: "What we agree upon is less important than that we all agree upon it!"[1]

The ability of the principal-in-charge to give legitimacy to the teachers decisions and work signifies perhaps the most important skill in enabling empowered teachers. Eileen describes this power to legitimize when she explains why she includes herself as a member of the problem-solving team:

> I know that some people say that we [principals] ought not even to be on these teams if we are really going to have shared decision making in schools—but it would be really misleading—even disempowering—to teachers to tell them

to go and make decisions that would be impossible to implement. You know, like one that was against board policy or one I know there isn't enough money for or one that is against some state regulation or something. If I am there when a decision is made, my presence sort of puts a stamp of legitimacy on it.

Put simply, even though teachers may have assumed the power to make decisions, someone with a broader knowledge base, that is, someone whose position offers a view beyond the classroom and instruction, needs to be there to indicate the feasibility of those decisions. If that someone is a principal-in-charge who has facilitated the teachers' empowerment from the start, the teachers can incorporate the principal's advice into the process.

And teachers do support the need for the principal's stamp of legitimacy. For example, when asked if she was worried about possible parent complaints, Sarah, an elementary school language arts teacher who is using some very innovative strategies to ensure inclusion of handicapped students in her classes in Alton Valley, an LRE study school, said about her principal, "Oh, Art thinks my project is fine! So, since he says it is okay, I don't expect any problems."

Enhancing Teacher Communication and Contact

Enabling teachers to develop leadership means that principals must support and provide opportunities for enhanced teacher contact and communication. Teachers are no longer isolated in classrooms or left to find time between classes to engage with other teachers. Teacher communication and contact are by-products of participatory decision-making forums and other in-service programs designed toward consensus building and goal development.

Teacher relationships must also evolve around the core technology of teaching and learning. Teachers who have collegial peer relationships are more likely to develop and accept changes (Little, 1982). Teachers "need time to talk with each other about the new procedures, to solve problems together and help each other learn how to be effective" (Leighton & Shaw, 1990). Through joint interactions, teachers can learn from each other how to improve their instructional practices and how to adopt these practices in the dynamic school. Collegial relationships also provide mechanisms for feedback that can help teachers press toward improvement (Rosenholtz, 1985). In addition, peer norms provide a mechanism to coordinate instruction and innovation within and across classrooms and grade levels of the dynamic school. Constructive teacher peer relationships are instances in which teachers meet together as leaders of their classrooms.

The principals-in-charge from the case study schools provide evidence of the work they do to enhance teacher communication and contact. Ken, the coalition principal, has made e-mail available to all teachers, and he reports that the majority of Midway's teachers are taking advantage of this method to connect with colleagues in other parts of the school, with himself, and with various bulletin services accessible through networks. Roger of the Central Middle School, a CAP school, scheduled shared-release times to enable collegial contact, and Larry touted the impact of having teams operating in the school: "People really talk with each other in our school—they don't hide in their classrooms. Because they work together so closely on the CAP teams, they have what I call an open door policy now. I intend to encourage more teams." Marsha, of the Littleton School, also noted one reason she facilitates the team approach: "My teachers aren't afraid of change—when the state sends some new mandate or something, they don't scream because they already have learned to solve problems by working together."

The responses from principals surveyed in the *High School and Beyond* study (USDE, 1984) provide further indication of their efforts to bring teachers together. The principals were asked to indicate the extent to which teachers work together in collegial peer relationships to help support joint efforts. We labeled their responses to a set of survey items (such as "the staff is continually evaluating its programs and activities" and "teachers are continually learning and seeking new ideas") *teacher press for improve-*

ment, that is, the extent to which teachers are mobilized to continual improvement in support of change.[2]

Using the teacher press for improvement scale, we asked whether
principals of dynamic schools in the *High School and Beyond* data
set report that their teachers engage in mutual contact aimed
toward school improvement more than their counterparts in traditional schools. The results indicate that principals in the data set
who work in dynamic schools—schools adopting numerous change
efforts—report more teacher press than do principals in static schools.
There is a positive, significant correlation between teacher press for
improvement and level of change. The more principals facilitate a
school climate that encourages teachers to press for school improvement through joint, collegial action, the more change practices are
adopted in the school. Changes in school practices occur more frequently when principals arrange supportive organizational conditions for teachers through norms of collegial press for improvement.

The *High School and Beyond* principals also indicated (on a
six-point Likert scale) the extent to which they emphasize various
collaborative activities with teachers when implementing school
improvement plans. In order from the greatest to the least emphasis
these activities include: (a) establishing clear, commonly accepted
school priorities and goals; (b) building a sense of community within
the school; (c) instituting systematic schoolwide staff development
activities linked to staff-identified needs and concerns; (d) promoting staff collaboration and collegiality; and (e) giving staff
responsibility for analyzing and solving school problems.[3]

On these five items, principals in dynamic schools differ from
principals of traditional schools. Principals implementing change
in the dynamic schools (i.e., principals-in-charge) institute systematic schoolwide staff development activities and emphasize
staff collaboration and collegiality more than their counterparts in
less dynamic schools.

The crucial point remains that the important task of the principal-
in-charge when facilitating teacher leadership is providing opportunities for teacher contact and communication around issues
that are facing the school. Teachers want to engage professionally with one another around issues of school improvement.

Principals-in-charge provide these opportunities through staff development activities, release time, and shared decision making.

Providing Rewards and Incentives for Teachers

Teachers who enlarge and redefine their roles must believe that their efforts lead to rewards, even if they are mainly intrinsic. Principals must realize the importance of reward, which include a sense of efficacy, a sense of personal growth, social interaction, and autonomy (Firestone, 1991). For instance, a heightened sense of self-efficacy or accomplishment is in itself rewarding. This follows Lortie's (1975) study, which found that teachers preferred the rewards that came with knowing they had reached a student. Conger and Kanungo (1988) suggest that initial empowering efforts should be aimed at providing successful experiences to teachers so they will gain a sense of efficacy. "Managers can structure organizational change programs in such a way that initial objectives are sufficiently attainable and subordinates are able to execute them successfully" (Conger & Kanungo, 1988, p. 479). Principals should stress outcomes of the empowering process, such as higher-quality decisions, more commitment to decisions, increased teacher input, and concrete changes as a result of participatory decisions. In short, participation should be intrinsically rewarding. In fact, past research suggests that teachers prefer task accomplishment to salary (Firestone, 1991).

Peer contact and increased professional interactions with principals can be viewed as rewarding for teachers; they are recognized as contributing professionals. These interactions also contribute to continued development. Principals can also use tangible rewards to recognize teachers who *are* teacher-leaders. Maeroff (1988) suggests that teachers should have to compete for admission to selective in-service programs so that selection itself serves as a reward.

Principals-in-charge must have the initiative and resources to reward teachers. By skillful use of these resources, principals can facilitate the work of teachers. Hence, another way for principals to facilitate teacher leadership is to employ differential rewarding for teachers who exert special efforts.

Principals responding to the *High School and Beyond* survey (USDE, 1984) were asked whether they use rewards for good teachers, such as giving time off for professional workshops, relieving teachers of administrative or disciplinary duties, and allowing teachers to choose the classes they teach.[4]

The results of our analyses from the *High School and Beyond* study indicate that principals in dynamic schools are more likely to use differential rewarding for teachers than are principals in static schools. There is a significant positive correlation between using rewards and adopting change practices.

Mobilizing Resources

For all of the above practices to succeed, principals must ensure that necessary resources are available. One of the most crucial resources is time. Principals must expand and redesign the use of time. Revising the teaching schedule is usually necessary if teachers are to have time to interact professionally. For example, in the Central Middle School, teachers who share the same students have a common work period in addition to their regular planning period. The principal worked with the central office and the unions to accomplish this restructuring of the schedule. Furthermore, principals must provide additional institutional support systems to promote teacher leadership, and this may require them to buffer these teachers from bureaucratic rigidity of other parts of the school system.

High-quality staff development and training must also be available. "Both symbolically and literally, in-service education must be moved out of dingy classrooms, and into the kinds of settings that signal to everyone that the activity is valued" (Maeroff, 1988, p. 475). These staff development opportunities must tackle normative and social conflicts that result as working relationships and roles are redefined (Hart, 1990).

Facilitating teacher leadership requires that teachers have time and contact with each other. Thus principals-in-charge must have the skills necessary to create resources and networks. Our case studies exemplify this point. A teacher in Marsha's school told us:

The skill to create these resources may look like magic, but Marsha does it! In her K-8 school, teams are able to free one partner to meet with their grade-level problem-solving team and to serve on a faculty-hiring team when one exists. Marsha also encourages her teams to use their contractually allowed personal/professional days to attend jointly professional conferences and workshops. They find a lot of time to talk—both in the car and between sessions. And they have shared a common experience.

Eileen's teachers may have thought she worked magic when she got funds from the school board to purchase enough trade books for the primary classes in her school:

I looked at the records from the [problem-solving] teams, and I saw that all the primary referrals were for reading problems. Well, I sit in those teams; I hear what the problems are. I knew that our basals were outdated and no good for those kids, with their language problems and all. So I took the team records to the board, and convinced them to allow us to use our text-replacement funds to buy appropriate trade books. That was not hard!

Roger, another principal-in-charge from the CAP data, created time when he set up a graduate course, offered at the school in late afternoons, when the district decided to change the school's designation to a middle school. He noted:

They needed the course for recertification anyway, but I really was not interested in the course content. I knew the professor was big on discussion, so I used this as time these folks could talk to each other and begin to shape for themselves what we were going to do.

Ken is among those principals who has discovered the computer as a way to link busy persons working in a large building. He has also sought and found foundation funding for substitutes to cover classes for teachers who meet as members of the planning team. Jim of the Hope Street School has the approval of the board and the union to offer compensatory time to those teachers who meet before or after school with their teacher assistance teams. Magic or manipulation, these principals-in-charge have created the resource of time for teachers to connect.

Summary

Principals-in-charge, like all principals, ensure that teachers can do their work by attending to the management of the building and by maintaining standard operating procedures. But principals in dynamic schools also establish organizational conditions that create and enable cohesive work groups that substitute for the direct, more autocratic leadership of a bureaucracy. Principals-in-charge support experimentation and risk taking through motivation and coordination.

The facilitating principal motivates and coordinates through a variety of ways. Symbolic acts, such as finding a small reward for a successful task force; political acts, such as asking the union president to speak at a meeting; structural acts, like providing substitutes to cover classes of teachers who are on a faculty-hiring committee are examples. These acts serve to encourage a collaborative and professional atmosphere, keeping the school moving forward together. They also legitimize teachers' work by saying, "Your work is important and accepted; you belong."

Principals-in-charge, then, accept the challenge to facilitate the internal leadership in their schools through effectively using a variety of skills. Just as Lee used the planning team, the teacher assistance teams, and the personnel search teams, principals-in-charge create arenas in which teachers actually influence the decisions that drive the internal operation of the school. In these arenas, the principals work to achieve real consensus among the participants. The task is not easy, but it is possible.

Principals-in-charge create resources and networks so that teachers have time and opportunities to connect and build collegial relationships, and have the support necessary to enact their decisions.

Lee, for example, found ways to release teachers for team meetings, to attend conferences together, and to connect through e-mail. Principals-in-charge motivate their faculties by providing support and rewards. Asking a teacher to speak at a community meeting, sending teachers to conferences, planning a surprise for a successful task force are some of the rewards Lee uses.

Finally, like Lee, who supports decisions made by the teachers in the school, the principals-in-charge legitimize the decisions and work of their faculty. Thus these principals enhance their teachers' sense of security and encourage them to take risks to grow and improve. In these ways, the principal-in-charge says, "My teachers are important to me, and I need and value their contributions to the leadership of this school." This stand enables the faculty to move toward a mutual vision for improving the school. In the next chapter, we see Lee in another crucial role, as the balancer, working within the system hierarchy.

Notes

1. Unless otherwise identified, the schools mentioned are from the CAP study. See Chapter 1 and the Appendix for information about this study and a complete list of all schools.

2. "Teacher Press for School Improvement" is a four-item Likert scale ($\alpha = 0.78$). The items included in this scale from the *High School and Beyond* survey are P35B, P35C, P35H, and P35J.

3. The questions from the *High School and Beyond* survey are P46L, P46K, P46E, P46J, and P46A.

4. The principals indicated whether they use different rewards from a list of 10 possible rewards. The reward scale is a factor-weighted mean of these 10 rewards ($\alpha = 0.66$), based on *High School and Beyond* survey questions P21B to P21H.

The Balancer

Communicating Within the System Hierarchy

Do principals of dynamic schools, principals-in-charge, have complete autonomy as they facilitate the internal functioning of their schools? As part of a complex hierarchy, they must be responsive to those working within their school, and they also are influenced by those higher in the educational system. In this chapter we look at Lee, who, to facilitate internally, must strike a balance between autonomy and hierarchical influence and control.

Marty looked over the latest draft of the planning council's proposal for an alternative schedule at Vibrant Springs. Lee had been keeping the superintendent apprised of each development in the council's progress. "I expect the board will go for this one—it's a far cry from the first schedule you threw at me. That one was pretty radical!" Marty commented.

"Well, we had to start some place, and I didn't want to put too many boundaries around what the group could do," Lee countered. "But, I agree, this plan is reasonable and workable. We've worked pretty hard and done a lot of soul searching about what we want in a schedule. I really am pleased with this version, finally. Still, I'm awfully glad I showed the earlier tries to you—

your insight did help. Besides, I know I wouldn't stand a chance with the board if you weren't behind it!"

"Okay," agreed Marty. "You have my support, and I'm not worried about board approval for this issue."

"Now," Lee continued, "I've got a favor to ask. This schedule, assuming it gets approved, means we'll be using teachers differently. Because we want teachers to work closely with small groups of students, we're going to be asking teachers to be responsible for more areas than those they may be certified in. Of course, they will have team members who are certified in those areas. I mean, kids will not be shortchanged. But I will need your help again with the state. We need relaxation of some of the certification requirements."

"And you think I can arrange that for you?" Marty laughed.

"Well, I'll write out the request to the state, but I need your backing. You can ease the way as you did when we wanted to integrate ESL, Chapter I, and resource into the regular class," Lee reminded Marty.

Marty laughed again. "What I like about you, Lee, is that you're not shy with me. You never hesitate to ask for what you want! Seriously, though, I'm glad you are direct because then I *know* what is going on. We can work together and not at cross-purposes, and I can always let you know any concerns I have. But then, I'll never forget the time you didn't warn me about that girl who hummed during the Pledge of Allegiance in the morning— when the calls and newspaper articles started, I wasn't quite prepared. I'm not sure I can ever forgive you for that one!"

"Yeah, what a learning experience that was! I didn't expect that would become so controversial—I didn't think it would go beyond my building," Lee said, groaning.

"If I'd known what the issue was, I probably could have predicted it—I've seen people get pretty emotional about things like the flag," Marty commented. "By the way, I'm glad you have gone ahead with that child advocacy group that wants to raise money for special activities. I hear you suggested they look into forming a nonprofit foundation."

"Yeah, I did want to fill you in on that one, but I think I know you well enough to assume that you'd like the idea." Lee smiled.

"The group has some strong people in it, so I'm trying to channel its energy into some concrete results. I sent the group members to talk to the people over in Littleton who have had some success with raising substantial amounts to fund their junior science program. I am meeting with the leaders of our group next week."

"One last thing before you go", Marty said. "Have you done any more thinking about your professional growth? You know, I think you are prime doctoral material."

"Ah, Marty, you know I want to go back to school. But how do I do it and be a principal, too? The logistics alone baffle me. Do you have any ideas?"

"That I may. Let's put this on the agenda for our next meeting. Your getting an advanced degree will benefit the district as well, so let's talk about it. Meanwhile, have a good day and see you at the board meeting," Marty responded.

* * *

Lee may be in charge of the school, but we see that Lee is not completely independent. To facilitate the school's internal workings, Lee must balance autonomy with central office influence and control. To some extent, Lee leads the school independently because of a strong and supportive relationship with the superintendent and the central office. Although these entities do not dictate Lee's actions inside the school, they do play an important part if the efforts of the principal-in-charge and the operation of the dynamic school are to be successful.

Because a dynamic school is engaged in collective decision-making processes, all members—teachers, administrators, students— articulate goals and missions, and plan strategies to meet these goals. Thus dynamic schools represent relatively autonomous, self-defining institutions. The facilitating principal-in-charge works toward establishing conditions within the school that enable work groups to function so they can move the total school toward improvement.

Principals of dynamic schools, however, are not totally autonomous and independent in their work. Like all principals, they function as both chief administrators at the school level and as subordinates to central office administrators; they are members of the organizational hierarchy. In this hierarchy, they must lead their schools according to numerous district and state policies. They interact with their superintendents and other central office personnel. The district as a whole is part of their context, and their actions are shaped by this context.

The relationship between the principal-in-charge and the superintendent and central office affects his or her interactions with important actors external to the school. Principals of dynamic schools recognize the importance of the superintendent's role as a link to other levels in the system hierarchy and, therefore, are careful to use that link to its fullest. For example, Lee's closeness with Marty eases interactions that the principal and the school may have with other governance bodies in the hierarchy such as the local school board and the state board of education. This closeness also frees the principal to deal with parents, the local press, and other community entities. Their shared vision provides an implicit approval from central office, which guides the principal when working with these groups and making decisions concerning community requests and interests.

This chapter develops the principal's role within the system hierarchy, explicating the relationship between the principal and superiors at the central office, focusing on the superintendent. Principals-in-charge choose to cultivate their roles as members of the system hierarchy to facilitate their own leadership, both internal and external to the school. They work collaboratively with central office personnel to foster a relationship of mutual respect, one that allows for a balance between autonomy and influence. Principals-in-charge realize that for a dynamic school to move toward improvement, the support and help of the central office personnel as partners, not adversaries, is crucial.

Correspondingly, principals of dynamic schools are aware of the complex, often difficult, conflict-ridden roles of the superintendent. Thus they help their superintendents perform successfully in their roles. An exchange relationship of mutual benefit develops based on challenge and support.

In sum, principals of dynamic schools not only lead the internal functioning of their schools but assume an active role within the hierarchy. They know it is essential to include diverse voices in school decisions, so they build a sense of community around common values and goals, forming a common bond of shared work (Bryk & Driscoll, 1988). One set of voices in this community comes from the superiors in the hierarchy. The principal-in-charge takes care to involve these actors as well as to manage the delicate balance between these voices and those internal to the school (i.e., teachers). Principals involved in change efforts actively coordinate and mediate the hierarchy's impact on the internal aspects of schooling so that all voices in the community may be heard.

Relationships Between Central Office and School Sites

The interrelationship between central office and local schools has been the subject of much thought and query. Practitioners and researchers have asked such questions as these: Who is primarily in a position to restructure schooling? Do districts influence what happens in individual schools, and if so, how? What is the nature of power, coordination, and control? (Crowson, 1988; Crowson & Morris, 1992; Cuban, 1989). Less is known about the role superintendents play in school effectiveness and improvement than the roles of teachers and principals (Wimpleberg, 1987), despite the prevailing view that central office administrators are crucial to school change processes (Fullan, 1982).

When school systems are conceptualized as loosely coupled (Weick, 1976) and/or as organized anarchies (March & Olsen, 1976), then it is predicated that the central office will have little impact on individual school sites and their principals. This view is supported by research that indicates that the central office has little control over teaching and learning activities (Hannaway & Sproull, 1978).

In contrast, it is widely believed that "instruction in most schools is not likely to improve unless a leadership consciousness at the district level develops in such a way as to forge linkages between schools and central office" (Wimpleberg, 1987, p. 106).

These linkages are direct, through rational processes, or indirect, through cultural-symbolic processes (Goldring & Hallinger, 1992). Sources of direct impact include specific district policies and rational-bureaucratic management. For instance, Murphy and Hallinger (1986) report that superintendents in instructionally effective districts carefully controlled goals, supervised and evaluated principals, were involved in staff selection, and focused curriculum and instruction in the district.

The district's impact on individual schools may be through cultural processes as well (Bolman & Deal, 1991; Fullan, 1991). District contexts influence schools through symbols, rituals, and common meanings (Firestone & Wilson, 1986).

> Over time, traditions and rituals—accepted ways of accomplishing the work of the organization—as well as shared values, evolve to create an ethos or culture in school districts. This cultural context acts as a control mechanism over the behavior of individuals and their work units (e.g. schools). (Goldring & Hallinger, 1992, p. 6)

Most likely schools are affected by both rational-bureaucratic and cultural mechanisms (Coleman & LaRocque, 1990).

The nature of the interrelationships between superintendents and principals and the ways in which these role partners influence one another have also been studied. Some suggest that relationships between superintendents and principals are driven by the conflictual nature of the superintendent's job and his or her need to manage risks (Crowson & Morris, 1992; Cuban, 1989; Hannaway, 1989). Hence, superintendents engage in administrative distancing between the central office and schools (Crowson & Morris, 1992). Simultaneously, they want open channels of communication and expect principals to keep them informed to prevent any surprises. Goldring's (1987) study of principals and parents exemplifies this point. She found that when interacting with parents, principals are concerned with confining parental complaints to the school site so they do not get to the superintendent. Thus principals act as buffers between the central office and parents. If they cannot buffer, they inform the superintendent in way of warning.

Principals, in turn, often look to superintendents for similar types of political help or buffering. For example, Goldring (1990) found that principals in high-status districts with volatile, demanding parental clienteles, are more likely to involve parents when they have close, frequent contact with their superiors at the central office and when the central office's policies are clear. This close contact with the central office reduces the principal's uncertainties and helps the principal feel less vulnerable vis-à-vis the parents. In other words, principals look to superintendents and district personnel to reduce uncertainties.

Others suggest these interrelationships may be based on misunderstandings of the other's role. For example, one study of superintendents and other school personnel in the state of Washington (Wolf, 1988) found that "what superintendents did or thought they did, and what principals thought they were doing, were quite different" (p. 22).

Principals' relationships with their superiors at the central office are shaped by both formal and informal control mechanisms (Crowson & Porter-Gehrie, 1980). Formal systems of influence and control are evident between principals and superintendents through the formal hierarchy even though principals may rarely be supervised or meet with central office personnel (Peterson, 1984; Wolcott, 1973). Control mechanisms include behavior controls, regarding issues such as teacher evaluation and curriculum, and output controls, according to student performance and public reaction. Formal controls serve as directive, restrictive, and/or formative forces for principals (Peterson, 1987).

Informal control mechanisms result from principals' dependencies on their superiors. Principals depend on the central office for such things as gaining resources for the school (i.e., extra computers) or developing a positive, widespread, professional reputation. This dependency provides superiors with considerable potential for influence over the principals, beyond formal mechanisms of control.

The changing structures of schools also provide new avenues for principal-superintendent interaction. School-based management and shared decision making, two school-improvement strategies that are being implemented widely, alter both the traditional formal and the informal control mechanisms in many districts. Principals in site-based management schools, although afforded more autonomy in planning and decision making, still must foster relationships with the remaining components in the system hierarchy. New demands and responsibilities emerge as crucial to effective school leadership. For example, as the authority for a larger domain of decisions devolves to the school site and as more stakeholders become involved in the decision-making process, a premium is placed on principals' human resource skills. They are expected to be more consultative and facilitative (Murphy & Hallinger, 1992).

Exacerbating this tension, these new groups involved in the decision-making process often bring with them different sets of values and interests. This highlights the need for principals with conflict resolution and consensus-building skills (Chapman, 1990). Effective principals also assume an educative leadership role to help the organization and its constituents learn, thus leading to more informal but higher-quality decisions (Duignan, 1990). In the latter capacity the principal assumes the role of "head learner" (Barth, 1990), an image that emphasizes the need for ongoing professional development for all in the schooling process.

Although principals are becoming more accountable to their school community with school-based management, they are still perceived as the primary school leader. These responsibilities result in significant role ambiguity (Chapman, 1990). A question remaining to be resolved is this: Who is accountable for decisions made under shared governance structures? Principals voice both hierarchical and nonhierarchical accountability concerns. From a hierarchical perspective, principals express the need for one individual who is ultimately accountable to the central office and board of education and resent being responsible for group-made decisions (Hallinger, Murphy, & Hausman, 1992). From a nonhierarchical viewpoint, principals question how shared governance meets the needs of parents who "don't want to come in and talk to a committee" but who are "interested in meeting with the person in charge" (Seeley, Niemeyer, & Greenspan, 1990, p. 14). Rizvi (1990) argues that this dilemma is best addressed by programs based on horizontal (e.g., peers, parents, and students) rather than vertical (e.g., educational bureaucracy) accountability.

Principals, in restructuring schools, report several additional concerns about the central office that they frequently view as an obstacle to fundamental reform. School heads express frustration over the reluctance of central office personnel to relinquish sufficient power to the school site so that school-based management can exert a real impact on students. The school's lack of authentic influence, principals say, diminishes the extent to which teachers are willing to be involved in the decision-making process. Ironically, despite decentralization, these principals describe an increase in central bureaucracy, which they view as an unnecessary demand on their already limited time available for instructional leadership roles (Hallinger & Hausman, 1993). Given these tensions, what role must the central office assume for restructuring to succeed?

If central offices relegate power to schools, it must be accompanied by innovative ways of thinking about leadership, involvement, and school improvement. Otherwise, bureaucracy merely relocates from the central office to the school site, with no new power being gained by school personnel and the community. It follows that the central office must assume a support role providing resources, technical assistance, and training that enables schools to succeed. In addition, practitioners note the necessity of a trusting environment, one in which schools feel safe taking risks and in which authentic influence is not undermined by central office dictates in areas where the site has been granted authority (Hallinger & Hausman, 1993). This is consistent with research in which principals identify superintendent leadership as mandatory for successful empowerment (Bredeson, 1989).

These descriptions of relationships between principals and their central office superiors create a basis for understanding the complex interactions that principals of dynamic schools have with their superiors. Although the principals-in-charge from our data sets all have strong relationships with their superintendents, these relationships are developed in typical district contexts of hierarchical power, conflict, and control. Unfortunately, principals are often judged by the extent to which they deal with problems without the involvement of the superintendent. Principals-in-charge, however, should work with their superintendents, despite the inherent difficulties of system hierarchies to build mutually beneficial interdependencies.

Dynamic Schools and the System Hierarchy

As we saw with Lee, the relationship between principals of dynamic schools and their superintendents is a strong one. Lee's confidence lies in the relationship built with Marty; this relationship frees Lee to build coalitions with other groups and to take calculated risks because Lee is sure of support from the central office. This support is not ungrounded—rather, it emerges from the constant communication, from the long hours spent discussing and sharing ideas. Because of this communication, the superintendent serves as a consultant, a resource, and a buffer. And the relationship works because it is a mutually beneficial one, with the principal keeping the superintendent informed and with both seeking to attain mutually defined goals.

Sharing and Defining Goals and Strategies

Principals-in-charge consult with their superintendents, seeking their perspectives and advice. Superintendents influence the decisions dynamic schools make. This is evident from our case studies and data from the *High School and Beyond* study (USDE, 1984). For example, Ken from the coalition school study, although perhaps an extreme example, considers Bob, his superintendent, to be one of his best friends. Bob's influence on Ken's actions is apparent when Ken's early plans for change are compared with those finally taken to the board. Ken brings his ideas or problems at their birth to Bob; they discuss and dissect, investigating possibilities and solutions. Bob's input clearly modifies the outcome, but the superintendent's involvement is not seen as infringement, because he has been a part from the beginning. Together, they shape the actions the principal will carry forward. This process was especially evident when Midway High School's planning team was preparing its restructuring model for board approval. Bob's advice was brought back to the team and ultimately led to workable modifications of the original plans.

Other examples of this close and supportive relationship between the principal-in-charge and the superintendent are found in the CAP data. Jim's superintendent Matt, although not actively involved in any day-to-day decisions, knew the ins and outs, ups and downs of the Hope Street School's classroom alternative support team. Thus when Jim came with the plan to offer compensatory time to team members for team service, Matt was able to approve the idea without further consideration. Similarly, Eileen's close relationship with Randy, her superintendent from Tipton, another CAP school, ensured his active support when she asked for trade books to replace old textbooks. In fact, because Randy was familiar with her team records, which were the basis for such a move, he helped her prepare her presentation to the board, and his introduction of her to the board left no room for doubt about where he stood on the request.

These cases were very different from the pilot district where CAP teams were floundering. At a superintendents' meeting, we discovered that the superintendent of this district was not even aware that his was a pilot district when he asked how he could get this program in his schools! Thus one of the contextual variables present in all schools where the classroom alternative support teams thrived and where inclusion efforts were attempted with some success was the presence of a supportive superintendent. In these cases, the superintendents were never surprised by the requests from their principals.

The *High School and Beyond* (USDE, 1984) data set also suggests that principals in schools engaging in change efforts are more likely to work with superintendents and central office personnel in school planning and decision making. Principals were asked to report the extent to which the superintendent and central office have actual influence on establishing the curriculum, determining instructional methods, and setting disciplinary policies.[1] The survey indicates principals of dynamic schools, those engaged in more change efforts, report that their superintendents and district office personnel have significantly more influence on establishing the curriculum, determining instructional methods, and setting disciplinary policies than do their counterparts in schools that are not engaged in as many change efforts.

Although this finding could be interpreted to indicate that principals of dynamic schools are less autonomous and are highly constrained by central office superiors, we believe that the data suggest that these principals have close relationships with their superiors at central office, such that the superintendent and others are involved in defining the core technology of the schools. To engage in change, principals need input from central office!

Exchanging Information

Principals-in-charge of dynamic schools and their superintendents are linked by the ongoing exchange of information. The principal serves as a source of information for the superintendent who is removed from the day-to-day operations of the school site. For example, Anita, an LRE school principal in Pete's district, commented, "I make sure that Pete knows. Usually I don't even want him to do anything about what I am telling him; I just want him to know what is going on." An example from Ken is when he informed Bob about a problem with a behaviorally disturbed boy, which Ken thought could be addressed by involving the boy's mother. "I called Bob first thing this morning. He told me to go ahead with my plan—I expected him to, but I still wanted him to know what I was going to do," Ken explains.

This information flow works both ways. Principals-in-charge recognize their superintendents as a resource. Superintendents have access to information that principals may not, and principals expect their central offices to share this information. Principals of dynamic schools count on their superintendents to get pertinent information to them quickly. Anita says, "Pete always lets me know what is coming down the pike—usually long before I have to do anything about it." Eileen remarks, "Thanks to Randy, I know the mood of the board. He lets me know if something about Tipton is going to surface, so that I can be there to deal with questions." Ken told us, "I count on Bob to tell me where I stand with the state, the board, with him. If he thinks I am operating out of my hip pocket, he lets me know."

Buffering From System Obstacles

Superintendents can facilitate principals to be in charge at the school site level by buffering them from external problems. By informing their principals about state and board policies or actions, superintendents help principals make site-specific decisions, thus buffering, or protecting, them from outside influences. This protection is correct, according to Goodlad (1984). He believes states should refrain from focusing on principals as accountable to the state. Rather the district is accountable to the state; therefore, each school and principal is responsible to the district central office. Goodlad supports a decentralization that gives power for decision making to the local school site within a framework of consistent and comprehensive goals designed to ensure equity and access.

The Re: Learning effort (a joint initiative between the Coalition of Essential Schools and the Education Commission of the States to secure support from statehouses for school restructuring) operates on this premise. The initiative asks states to relax regulations for individual schools as long as the schools continue to meet carefully articulated goals.

The Cotter School, a school trying to establish a Least Restrictive Environment (LRE) for its handicapped students, illustrates one state's willingness to flex regulations. Certain state certification requirements were suspended to allow teachers to work with alternative groupings. Hugh, the principal, was responsible to his central office. Problems that did arise were largely the result of internal failures, not because of interference from the state.

In sum, principals of dynamic schools from our data sets shared goals and missions that they had defined jointly with their superintendents. Ken describes Bob in these roles: "I count on him playing the devil's advocate. I know he will find a way to help me do most anything if I've really thought it out, but he really makes me do my homework!" Because principals-in-charge do their homework, they are able to balance their need for independence and the need for resources and influence from the central office. Because both are part of a complex system, superintendents and principals-in-charge are able to work as a team to achieve their mutually defined goals, each with separate, albeit interacting, functions.

Summary

Principals of dynamic schools value, rather than rail against, their relationships within the complex hierarchy of public education. They know they benefit from the information and support that comes from a close link with their superintendents and central offices. This closeness better enables them to facilitate the internal workings of the school—the teaching and the learning, the team operations, the teacher leadership, the student and teacher interactions, and the volunteer functions, to name a few. It also better equips them to deal with the community in which the school resides—the parents and various parent groups, the businesses, and the agencies.

We have seen that Lee and Marty are working to achieve the same ends—an improved learning environment for all students, which taps the resources of the community to its fullest. They work in tandem, not at cross-purposes, because they share similar visions. They do not always agree on operational details, but they are always willing to discuss their differences and to hear the other's perspective. Lee's responsibility is to flesh out and enact that vision; Marty's role is to encourage, to procure resources when possible, to identify limits, and to hold Lee accountable.

But principals-in-charge maintain independence within the hierarchy so that their schools may address appropriately those needs unique to themselves. They know their schools cannot simply be automatic cogs in the system, reacting only to directives from above. They and the other internal leaders within the building must make decisions about the goals and objectives for their schools as well as the daily operations of their buildings based on their unique and self-defined missions. Thus we have labeled the role of the principal-in-charge within the system hierarchy *the balancer*. We believe this term describes best the challenge to these principals who must be responsive to those above and below in the hierarchy as well as a variety of other constituencies. As balancers, they walk a line between independence and dependence, between autonomy and external influence. Principals of dynamic schools succeed as balancers by defining and establishing a strong and mutually beneficial relationship with their superintendents and central offices. Their challenge is to strike this balance.

Note

1. The analyses are based on *High School and Beyond* survey questions P32B1, P32C1, P32B2, and P32C2.

The Flag Bearer and Bridger

Managing the Environment

How have changes in society and in restructured schools altered the nature of the relationships between principals and their constituencies? In this chapter we see how these changes link schools more directly with their environments and increase the influence of the external environment on the management and control of the internal functioning of the school. We see that Lee acknowledges this link and uses it to the school's benefit.

Alma handed Lee the schedule for the day. "Looks like you'll be running all day. Do you have time for a cup of coffee before you meet with the SAEC [Southeast Asian Education Council]?"

"Not really, because I should call Mrs. Thomas before I leave. Did she say what she wanted?"

"Yes, she's concerned that her daughter might not be getting the right kind of English. She wants to know, as she put it, 'What's the story on all this process writing stuff?' She said she had to check it out with you—that she'd take your word it's okay."

"She just needs reassurance that Mrs. Minto knows what she is doing. I'll take care of that."

The SAEC meeting would not be as easy. Lee wondered what was the best action. So many Southeast Asian immigrants had flooded the community in the past decade. As the children became Americanized, teen gangs began to form. Lee had chosen not to ignore their emergence. Consequently, Lee approached the Southeast Asian community leaders and was glad they had responded with concern. The community formed an education council about a year ago, and this council had proposed a separate, albeit temporary, school program for their youngsters. Although opposed to any form of segregation, Lee understood the council's motivation—an attempt to maintain traditional values. This morning's meeting would address that proposal. Whatever the outcome, Lee and the school were involved.

At some time during the morning, Lee needed to call the sales rep from a local toothpaste company to refuse their offer to provide a fluoride treatment for students to rinse with every morning in school. "That's one opportunity I choose to turn down. I expect the teachers would view the procedure as a disruption."

Next, Lee noted that lunch was scheduled with some officers of the First National Bank. Lee had been courting this bank, located just down the road from Vibrant Springs, for financial support for some special projects in the school. Then, after lunch, the planning team would be meeting. The topic would be eliminating the gifted program, and Lee intended to propose that the team arrange a meeting with the parent advisory council to explain the rationale. The parent reps on the planning team indicated that any action to do away with the program would get some heat from parents of kids in the program. Lee hoped to head off any divisive protest through early parental input, but Lee also realized some negotiation might be necessary.

Later that afternoon, Lee would meet with Tony and Moira Calabretta. They had accepted Lee's request to head the formation of a Vibrant Springs community education foundation. Across the country, communities were forming such nonprofit foundations to raise money to support school programs that taxes could no longer cover. Lee knew the community had a strong constituency that could offer additional financial support to the school, and the Calabrettas seemed a viable link to that group.

The day would not be over until Lee spoke at the Taxpayers' Association annual dinner that evening. Lee had accepted their invitation, seeing this as an opportunity to share Vibrant Springs's mission with a large group. "Unless the community understands what we are about, we cannot expect their support.

"Yes, the day will be a long one, and how different from one of several years ago," Lee thought. "Today will be a day where my efforts are all directed outward, to ensure support inward."

* * *

In the previous chapters we saw that because Lee's school was changing internally the principal behaved differently from a principal of a traditional school. Lee has established strong linkages with Marty, the superintendent, and the central office, linkages that have enabled Lee to be a principal-in-charge of a dynamic school. Within the school, Lee facilitates the other adults to take on many of the leadership functions previously relegated to the principal alone. With shared decision making and teacher leadership, Lee is relieved of some of the specific functions that had fallen only to the principal. Because Lee's role inside the school is largely that of the facilitator, Lee is able to place more focus on many of the external forces playing on the school than Lee's counterpart in a more traditional school is. At the same time, these external forces are requiring that Lee attend to the community demands and resources. With the internal work of the school reorganized, then, Lee can and must spend time and energy dealing with the external tensions, nurturing the school's relationships with the world outside its walls.

The need for Lee to focus on external relationships is critical. Dissatisfaction with public schools throughout the country has been driving school reform. The recent reform efforts and calls for school restructuring are altering the external boundaries of schools and thereby affecting the nature of the relationships between principals and their constituencies. Principals-in-charge recognize the need to include parents and other community members to make decisions, mobilize resources, measure accountability, and recruit and retain students and teachers. All of these changes are linking schools more tightly with their community and ultimately increasing the impact of the external environment on the management and control of the internal functioning of schools.

Spanning the Boundaries

We base this chapter on the assumption that principals of dynamic schools must pay increased attention to managing the external environment of their schools and, consequently, must define their roles in terms of spanning the boundaries between the internal school functioning and the external environment. When referring to the school's environment, we mean all elements existing outside the boundary of the school that can have an impact on all or part of the school (Daft, 1983).

In Chapter 4, we discussed the relationship between principals and their superiors within the school governance hierarchy, that is, directly with the superintendent and central office and indirectly with the school board and state department of education. In this chapter, we focus on the external environment, or the community, including parents, businesses, agencies, and other groups in the community.

Old boundaries separating the school from the community have been destroyed, and new ones have been defined. We credit the forces in the environment described in Chapter 1 as well as reform and restructuring efforts with these changes. Principals-in-charge engage in boundary-spanning activities and guide their schools using environmental management strategies, because only those schools that adapt sufficiently to their new environments will flourish in the new circumstances created by a changing context (Goldring, 1986).

Principals-in-charge accept the boundary-spanning function and proactively engage in managing the environment. They define the important dimensions of the external environment, then develop and implement boundary-spanning activities both to respond to and to create positive environmental forces. Principals-in-charge are those principals who either build a niche for their schools in the ecology of the environment or who seek alternative environments for their schools. They take on the roles of negotiator and communicator, explicitly explaining and publicizing the school's mission and relevant programs to community constituencies while developing and nourishing external support. Thus they are both political and symbolic leaders. They build bridges between the school and the surrounding worlds and then bear the school's flag across those bridges. They transmit what the school stands for, and they maneuver for strength, independence, and resources in a competitive world. To meet this increased need to manage the environment, principals-in-charge must balance their roles as the facilitator of internal processes with those of the boundary spanner.

Although boundary spanning is an important activity for the school organization in the age of school reform and restructuring, we acknowledge that principals are somewhat limited in their actions regarding the environment. They do, however, have considerable latitude for making choices. Because environmental problems are difficult to solve, a leader can choose to ignore them or to be defensive about their existence. A principal-in-charge, on the other hand, is not reluctant to tackle these problems. In other words, principals such as Lee recognize and deal directly with the contexts in which their schools operate. They recognize that their organizations are externally constrained and controlled by their environments as a result of their dependencies on the environment for survival, such as receiving budget allocations and quality teachers. At the same time, they try to manage these dependencies, to adapt to environmental demands, and to retain discretion and autonomy over the school's internal activities.

But, how does a principal-in-charge bridge the external worlds and build new relationships? What are the strategies that a principal-in-charge uses to manage the school's external environment? Principals-in-charge engage in ongoing, boundary-spanning activities that not only link the school to the environment but also promote long-term policies and activities that include the environment.

In managing the school's environment, Lee uses various strategies. Some may be used with the intent of increasing school and community interactions, whereas other strategies are intended to reduce such relationships. Principals of dynamic schools have an eye to the external. They use varied approaches to engage with the school's environment. In this chapter, we explore these strategies by seeing how principals of dynamic schools manage their environments. To this end, we ask, "What environmental management strategies do principals-in-charge use?"

Environmental Management Strategies

Principals of dynamic schools are leaders who bridge the boundaries between their organizations and the environment; hence they assume the role of boundary spanner. They must employ complex strategies that require broad-based planning and action to respond to and capitalize on their changing, turbulent environments. These strategies are tools principals of dynamic schools use to help their schools learn about, adapt to, and modify their environments.

Environmental management strategies can be grouped into two broad categories: responding to the environment and maintaining relationships with the environment (Table 5.1). The first strategy, responding to the environment, often involves approaches that are crucial in the process of changing a school from a traditional school to a dynamic school engaged in change efforts. This set of strategies refers to efforts by which the school will change its structures and processes as a result of environmental contingencies, such as state mandates for change or community needs. Responding to environmental concerns, schools restructure through organizational redesign to adapt better to present environmental contingencies and broaden and change their environment and constituencies by altering the mission through strategic maneuvering. These two strategies, organizational redesign and strategic maneuvering, are used to change the school to facilitate school-environment relations.

The second environmental management strategy, maintaining the school's relationships with its environment, includes approaches to manage external relationships that are ongoing and routine; they are strategies used within the existing school and environmental context. These include strategies aimed at reducing the interdependencies, interrelationships, and interactions between the

Table 5.1 Strategies for Managing the Environment

Responding to Environmental Contingencies	Maintaining Relationships With the Environment	
Organizational Redesign Strategic Maneuvering	Promoting Independence:	public relations volunteering buffering
	Promoting Connections:	cooperation contracting cooptation coalition building socialization

school and its environment and strategies directed toward continuous school-environment cooperation and adaptation.

Responding to Environmental Contingencies

Principals-in-charge, like Lee, operate in schools that are products of a major strategy to respond to external environments. Because they are leaders of dynamic schools, they direct their schools in efforts of *organizational design* (Kotter, 1979), which is "the process of grouping activities, roles, or positions in the organization to coordinate effectively the interdependencies that exist" (Pfeffer & Salancik, 1978, p. 25). Organizational design strategies aim at restructuring the organization to adapt to the environment. Consequently, a crucial environmental management strategy is to alter design features of the school to allow the school to survive in particular environmental circumstances, especially when the demands from the environment for such efforts are widespread. Schools that are responding to external demands for change often are restructured schools; they restructure through organizational design.

From the principal's viewpoint as external leader, finding the best fit between the school's organizational design and its external environment is imperative. Burns and Stalker's (1961) seminal research suggests a pattern of congruence that reflects this type of environmental fit. Their study of 20 manufacturing organizations indicated that those organizations facing relatively stable environments resembled mechanistic structures. Mechanistic structures are characterized by rigid task definitions, formalization of authority, vertical communication patterns, and centralized control mechanisms. In contrast, organizations in rapidly changing, dynamic environments resembled organic structures. These structures are characterized by flexible task definitions, low formalization of authority, lateral communication patterns, and diverse control mechanisms.

The schools in our studies face changing and complex external environments; their structures are already organic or were becoming organic in response to these external demands. For example, Midway, Ken's school, chose to restructure and join the coalition to meet the needs of all its students. Ken acknowledged that the school population had changed over the last decade as voluntary busing had brought African-American students out from the inner city and as the economic level of families living in the section of the district Midway served had dropped. The school's effort to eliminate tracking is one example of a change specifically aimed to enhance Midway's ability to serve its increasingly diverse student body.

Similarly, changes that include a parent's library at the Willowtree School are designed to address community needs. A parent in the Willowtree community comments on the changes since Anita came to the school: "I know she really cares; for the first time I believe that someone will listen to me!"

Principals of dynamic schools often choose environmental management strategies that try to change, alter, or broaden the environment. By redefining the school's goals and programs, they create alternative, broader environments for their schools. These strategies, designed to influence the nature of the school's environment are labeled *strategic maneuvering.* In the corporate world, mergers are one example of strategic maneuvering procedures. Other examples of strategic maneuvering are changing physical location and diversifying.

In schools, principals achieve strategic maneuvering by defining new missions, such as developing a specific specialty or theme, as in a magnet school. This strategy helps the school to broaden the ways in which it meets the needs of the community and often allows the school to begin to attract a totally new type of student body. Capitalizing on their knowledge and connections with the environment in which the school is embedded, principals are central to making decisions about the types of programs to be offered and to ensuring proper coordination and linkage between the school and its constituencies. Because community input does play a role in the decision-making process of a dynamic school, the task for the principal as environmental leader becomes even more complex in these schools. Domains of the different constituencies must be defined and their interface coordinated.

Principals-in-charge learn from the external environment to acquire the inputs needed both to meet the demands of their environments and to broaden and change their mission. Having defined their schools' domains and established their legitimacy, these principals act as entrepreneurs; they use their knowledge about and their relationships with the environment to mobilize resources and to develop new projects to sustain the school.

The principals of dynamic schools from our data sets were entrepreneurs. Ken sought external funding by carrying the school's defined mission to a foundation and to a regional corporation. Art, an LRE principal, lunched often with local banking officials and businesspeople to keep the school visible and connected to the community. Every year, Anita saw that one of her teachers wrote a proposal on behalf of the schools for the Grants for Principals program sponsored by the local foundation.

Principals-in-charge take control of their environments through organizational redesign inside the school and strategic maneuvering. Our dynamic schools that are having success with LRE are responding to environmental demands (i.e., the federal and state mandates and parental pressure) to integrate students with needs into regular classrooms. An LRE principal, Mike specifically notes that parents are the driving force behind the LRE activities. Many of our CAP principals use the teams as a maneuver to bring solutions to student learning and behavior problems back into the realm of regular education within the school. Similarly, when Ken's school chose to join the Coalition of Essential Schools, it redefined its mission, thereby realigning and widening its support system outside the school.

Maintaining Relationships With the Environment

Once organizational redesign and strategic maneuvering are completed, and schools have responded to their environments, these new relationships need to be maintained. At times, the principal-in-charge wants to allow the school to function more independently from external input. Independent strategies are aimed at reducing environmental influence on the school. "The independent strategies are means by which the organization can reduce the uncertainty and/or dependency which may threaten its existence by drawing on its own resources and ingenuity" (Galbraith, 1977, p. 204). Independent strategies allow the school to maintain a certain amount of self-control in light of its dependencies on the external environment.

Principals of dynamic schools tend to choose from among three independent environmental management strategies. Most frequently, principals of dynamic schools use the *public relations response*. Public relation strategies attempt to control and manage the school environment by influencing the environment's perceptions of and knowledge about the school. Principals use this strategy to attract support and resources as well as to retain students and staff. Schools vary in the amount of expenditure and effort on public relations, but Thompson (1967) suggests that this strategy helps organizations gain prestige at a relatively low cost.

Principals of dynamic schools take charge of environmental information as they link the school with the community to facilitate the public relations role in the external environment. They are exposed to large amounts and types of information. Principals as boundary spanners filter this information and decide who needs to receive what information. Hence, they serve as filters and facilitators and disseminators (Aldrich & Herker, 1977). Some information is stored for later use, some is immediately passed on to other units for processing, and other information is acted on autonomously by the boundary spanner. For example, a principal of a dynamic school has access to more information than do the members of the school decision making teams; the principal-in-charge decides what information will be most useful to which group. By controlling information, principals can protect the school from stress and other external interferences and can strategically assess potential decisions and their impact on the public relations image of the school.

Boundary spanners collect information by constantly scanning their environments through various modes (Daft, Sormunen, & Parks, 1988). Galaskiewicz and Wasserman (1989) report that managers use personal scanning modes, which include direct face-to-face interactions such as meetings, to gather information about how to relate to their environments. Our principals-in-charge thus use public appearances in the community more than written communication. Daft and colleagues (1988) report that managers tend to use these personal modes for scanning because environmental conditions are changing and unstable.

When environments are rapidly changing and unstable, firm data are difficult to obtain. Thus Daft and colleagues (1988) also found that high-performing firms, defined by profitability, used scanning more frequently than did low-performing firms. Scanning for information is an especially critical role for boundary spanners who are attempting to deal with environmental uncertainty when decisions are being made and policy being formed.

Principals of dynamic schools use environmental scanning to collect the necessary information to influence strategic policy-making, planning, and public relations. Again, the principal is in charge because he or she has access to multiple sources of information and then chooses to filter and disseminate it in ways that serve to shape the organization. Because the principal is making the choices about what and how information is to be used, the principal as a boundary spanner has a crucial role in defining the school's goals and mission and ensuring smooth interaction with the environment according to these goals. Thus such a principal is both a flag bearer and a bridger.

Several of our principals from the CAP, LRE, and Coalition case studies offer specific illustrations of principals using information and promoting public relations. All were, in some way, information collectors and users. We have already met Eileen who routinely scanned the record sheets from problem-solving teams to detect any changes in the student body that might reflect changes in the environment; in this way, she discovers potential language and reading problems emerging from an influx of immigrants. Ken's daily walks through Midway flood him with information about the environment, and his networking through e-mail with the town government's news bulletin keeps him abreast with local events and policy initiatives. Ken filters this information, making choices about where he believes it will be most useful.

Marsha accomplishes both information collection as well as information bearing in her bimonthly lunches as a member of the local Rotary Club in Littleton. Paul, another CAP school principal, regularly plays golf with friends in the community. "Sure, I do it for fun, but I can't say that I don't keep my ears open all the time. That's how I found out that the taxpayers were ready to support the school addition. I don't always use the information myself—sometimes I just pass it along if I think it will help us get where we want to go," he explains.

Mike of the Stewart School, both a CAP and a LRE school, illustrates the principal-in-charge who scans and chooses. Among the advocacy groups whose voices he heard, Mike chose to respond to the parents of handicapped children who were supporting the inclusion movement. Together, they proposed to the school board a plan for alternative groupings with aide support.

Contact with parents is part of the principal's information-gathering role. Interactions with parents provide the principal with crucial information. Principals responding to the *High School and Beyond* (USDE, 1984) survey were asked questions about the frequency of their interactions with parents.[1] Data analyses revealed that principals in dynamic schools report meeting more often with parents than do principals in traditional schools. Furthermore, these dynamic principals report that parents contact the school regarding their children more frequently than do principals in traditional schools.

As boundary spanner, the principal maintains the legitimacy of the school in the eyes of the community by transmitting the proper types and amount of information to it about school functioning (Aldrich & Herker, 1977). Maintaining the school's visibility enhances this connection between the school's goals and its constituencies.

Principals of dynamic schools choose to spend time and energy on public relations as an environmental management strategy. Because parents and other community members continually pass judgment on the school's internal operations, usually without adequate information, an effective principal recognizes the power in providing information to shape these judgments. Through public relations, the principal creates an image for the school that people can believe in. The image says, "This is who we are, and what we stand for is positive. Support us." Thus principals-in-charge try to influence their communities through information dissemination and advertising.

Dynamic schools commonly use another independent external management strategy, the *voluntary response*. A voluntary response occurs when the school responds to needs in the external environment more than is necessary or generally expected. Dynamic schools often choose a voluntary response out of a sense of social responsibility, such as hiring disadvantaged groups from the school community as a means of supplying them with employment. Furthermore, they automatically use a voluntary response when they involve parents and community members as part of teams and committees. This environmental management strategy is a way to increase the satisfaction of the environment of the school and to enhance school-environment relations. The voluntary response is a strategy that can counterbalance dissatisfactions in other areas (e.g., criticisms of low achievement) or can be used at a later date when resources and support are scarce.

In many cases, principals may prefer to reduce environmental influence as much as possible, that is, to seal off the school from environmental influences. This strategy is termed *buffering* (Thompson, 1967), and various buffering strategies are available. For example, buffering may be used to reduce the amount of interference caused by parents. This is usually achieved by creating formal procedures to deal with parental requests. Principals who insist that parents contact them first before confronting a teacher are buffering the teachers from the parents. Hollister (1979) found that schools with high parental demands adopt rationalistic, bureaucratic controls to deflect these demands. In a dynamic school, this strategy may be adopted informally as a means to protect teachers, because the parents already see the principal as the legitimate authority. For example, in the Alton Valley School, Sarah noted that parents tended to check out anything new with her principal, Art, first because he had built trust with parents. Obviously, buffering strategies if used alone have their cost because the source of the vulnerability (i.e., the parents) is not removed and no attempt is made to control the cause of the immediate problem to reach long-term solutions.

Once again, the principals from our case studies illustrate the use of independent strategies. Marsha fought to maintain the hiring of all school aides from within the community. Art employed a parent volunteer to coordinate press releases for the local newspaper; this parent had previously been in the public relations business. The Cotter School parents understood that they were to come to Hugh, the principal, first with any questions. Hugh also was explicit about his efforts to filter any requests from local business, agencies, or other groups. He tells about the time when he refused to allow the playground group to ask teachers to coordinate the children's selling of magazine subscriptions: "While it may have been for a good cause, I saw a source of major conflict in the arrangement, so I just made the choice not to allow the group to approach the teachers. I felt I could deal with their initial annoyance easier than I would be able to handle all the problems that could arise later."

Not all our principals successfully employed independent strategies, indicating the importance of these strategies. Ken, while he believed he was communicating with important constituencies, failed to reduce environmental influence when his planning team proposed the elimination of the honors classes. Insufficient public relations or inadequate buffering resulted in a vocal opposition group's near-success at blocking the proposal's implementation.

Principals-in-charge use independent environmental management strategies and buffering to respond to the environment through self-control. That is, the school acts to increase its own independence and status in relation to its environment. In contrast to independent strategies, principals of dynamic schools choose cooperative strategies when their aim is to increase the cooperation and joint action between the school and the environment. Cooperative strategies generally require that the school relinquish some autonomy to adapt to its environment.

Although most schools use *implicit cooperation,* that is, they act in tandem with elements in their environment without explicitly trying to coordinate behaviors, dynamic schools often use a more planned cooperative strategy: *contracting.* When the school negotiates directly with elements in the environment to reach an explicit agreement, a contract of cooperation occurs. Usually, contracting follows a lengthy exchange of information and communication. Contracts allow schools to coordinate future activities with environmental elements in a changing environment (Scott, 1981). An example of a contract is when a local business agrees to donate a certain set of supplies throughout the school year.

Although contracting creates certainty and predictability, it often results in loss of autonomy and a great investment in time and energy for the school organization. Contracting allows elements in the environment, whatever business or entity is involved, to have influence in the decision-making processes of the school. Contracting is involved when schools make arrangements with specific agencies to provide services, such as those to students with special needs. Our CAP schools, for example, often report contracting with external experts for therapy or testing services. Usually, this type of contracting implies joint planning and decision making about the curricula and level of instruction for these students.

Three other forms of cooperation that principals of dynamic schools use on a regular basis are *cooptation, coalition building,* and *socialization.* The principal joins elements from the school and the environment for a common purpose in these closely related strategies. Each unit retains its independence, and the school retains some control over the means used to achieve the common goals with their environmental partners (Corwin, 1965).

In the coalition arrangement, mutual action and commitment unite decision making (Thompson, 1967). Because the school will not act without consulting its external coalition partner, this strategy affords the partner considerable inclusion in the school's processes.

For example, coalition forming, aimed at complete cooperation between the school and the parents, is used when principals and parents work together to achieve common goals. In this case, principals view parents as important allies with similar aims and interests and seek to involve them. The productivity of the coalition stems from the members sharing a common perspective on particular issues (Scott, 1981).

In contrast, cooptation is the process of absorbing elements from the environment into the school organization to reduce threats. Unlike coalition building, "the strategy of cooptation involves exchanging some degree of control and privacy of information for some commitment of continued support from the external organization" (Pfeffer, 1972, p. 222). Through cooptation, schools establish linkages with elements in the environment on which they are highly dependent (Pfeffer, 1972). Incorporating parents or other community representatives into the decision-making processes of the school may exemplify cooptation.

The cost of cooptation to the school is great. Elements from the environment gain control and influence concerning the internal functioning of the school. Coopted elements have more influence than do those elements involved in a contracting relationship with organizations, because cooptation allows influence over a wide range of activities and topics, whereas contracting is usually confined to specific domains. Consequently, it seems that cooptation may be used when other environmental management strategies are not sufficient.

Cooptation is beneficial to the school because the school has control over the environmental element more than would be the case if it were completely outside the school's realm of norms and authority. In fact, often the coopted element begins to identify with the school and therefore becomes less of an adversary. Furthermore, having taken part in the decision-making processes of the school, the coopted element may show commitment to the policies that were formed. For example, principals generally coopt parents through dominating the PTA and using it as a support group for their own decisions (Gracey, 1972; Vidich & Bensman, 1960; Wolcott, 1973).

In practice, differentiating between coalition building and cooptation is difficult. For example, when our CAP schools regularly seek parental involvement as one intervention to improve student learning, the goal may be either cooptation or coalition building. The schools may either view the parents as true, equal partners or as external elements to placate.

Similar to, but less formal than, cooptation as a type of coop-eration between schools and their environments is *socialization*. In this strategy, the principal and school work to bring all elements of the environment into accepting the schools norms, values, and operating procedures. Although the aim is shared values among elements, no formal role is given to the elements representing the environment. Principals engage in socialization as they try to channel and mold parental involvement into acceptable and man-ageable styles by creating congruence between the school's resources and parental expectations. Through socialization, principals try to encourage parents to accept the school's goals and methods as they "de-educate the public about the school's capabilities and re-educate it about what it can reasonably expect from the school" (Morris, Crowson, Porter-Gehrie, & Hurwitz, 1984, p. 116).

Our principals-in-charge commonly use cooperative strate-gies. Ken always included representatives from parent or commu-nity groups on any school decision-making teams, Marsha made sure that parents were included on the strategic planning team established for her school, Mike even had a parent on his problem-solving team. Roger's school contracted with the regional special education service to provide specific assistance for children with special needs. Paul's school regionalized with several others in adja-cent small communities to formalize their relationships. On the other hand, although he did bring in speakers and hold workshops, Ken's attempts to socialize all parent constituencies to accept the changes he was working to implement were not always successful.

Summary

In a dynamic school, the principal is not the only person to carry out environmental management and boundary spanning. Boundary-spanning roles are highly cross-functional (Hambrick, 1981). Some boundary roles (i.e., collecting information) are car-ried out by many people in an organization, whereas other roles are carried out only by specific individuals. Shared decision mak-ing places some responsibility for boundary-spanning activities in the hands of teams and teacher-leaders. For example, both principals and teachers gather information from parents, and although principals usually are the ones to engage in resource mobilization, specific teams in a dynamic school may focus on this task.

Principals of dynamic schools, then, are not the only persons visible in the school environment, but as internal facilitators, it falls to them to coordinate these external roles. The principal-in-charge delegates and oversees boundary role functions in the total school organization. The principal-in-charge scans and chooses, filters and facilitates, seeks and develops. As boundary spanners, such principals act as monitors, disseminators, and spokespersons.

These principals see their work as extending beyond the boundaries of the school, bridging the internal world of the school with the environment. Taking charge of information, they truly are principals-in-charge. They gather information and make decisions about how to use it. By making such decisions, they enhance the school's definition and its mission for all constituencies, both internally and externally. They facilitate connections between as well as within, promoting a total school climate that supports change.

Principals of dynamic schools do have degrees of control over their environments. As leaders with their eyes to the external environment, they maintain their relationships with the environment through routine boundary-spanning activities. They choose from various strategies to manage their relationships with the environment. First, schools respond to environmental constituencies through redesign and strategic maneuvering, and then they manage their external relationships with independent and cooperative strategies.

Looking at all the strategies collectively, we see that they are aimed at striking a workable balance between increasing school-environment interactions and reducing such relationships. Changing the school's design structure and cooperating with the environment will create the most open relationship with the environment, whereas buffering and maneuvering into another domain will create the least amount of interactions with the present environment. Although changing the internal aspects of the school can prove costly, difficult, and complex, this type of restructuring allows for meaningful change efforts.

Clearly, principals-in-charge do not always use a single strategy, and strategies are related. By definition, they deal with organizational design because dynamic schools are ones that have chosen to restructure. Their redesign may later lead them to redefine their environments. In some situations, they may choose to cooperate with the community; in others, buffering certain school functions from the community may be the best approach. What differentiates principals of dynamic schools from other principals is their awareness and conscious choice to interact with and manage their environments using these boundary-spanning and environmental management tools. These are principals who facilitate their school's definition and then carry that definition outside the boundaries of their schools, seeking support and strength to carry out their school's mission. They are the flag bearers and the bridgers.

Note

1. The questions correspond to the *High School and Beyond* survey questions PO4 and PO5.

The Inquirer

Assessing Effectiveness and Developing School-Based Accountability

How do principals-in-charge evaluate their schools? How can they evaluate their own work as leaders of dynamic schools? And how can other stakeholders measure the school's effectiveness? How are school outcomes related to the principal's performance? In this chapter, we look at Lee, the evaluator—of self and of the school. Because of new roles, the principal's role in accountability must be seen in a new light.

"So, how *do* we know you are doing a good job as principal? How do we know that Vibrant Springs School is achieving what we want?" Marty, the superintendent, asked Lee during lunch. It was the day after a board meeting on personnel evaluation. Linda Alfonte, the board chair, had asked specifically about Lee's work because Lee was seen as "doing things somewhat different from what we are used to." Alfonte had gone on to say, "Not that we disapprove, but, you know, we have relaxed some of our policies for you to try some new approaches, and yet I don't know that we've seen student scores increase. The union hasn't complained, so I see that as a good sign. Still, we need results. You tell us that this restructuring is working, and we have agreed to support your change efforts, but now we need to know if you are really running the school as well as you should be. What *are* you doing? We need to know if you are an effective principal."

"Obviously, I believe you are doing a good job—no, make that a great job," said Marty, "but their request for documentation is legitimate. And other groups want to know as well, so we need to develop an evaluation plan that will show what you really are doing at Vibrant Springs. Otherwise, people will base their evaluation solely on student achievement scores." Marty pointed out that, although he held annual performance evaluation conferences with each administrator, the discussions were based on data he had informally collected and applied to his criteria and standards. "Let's talk about how we can best assess your performance, given what you are trying to do."

Lee agreed, "It would help me if we systematically gathered information that really tells me where my strengths and weaknesses are. What I'm trying to do is create an environment in which all kids can learn, but student outcome scores alone won't tell me much about the difference *I* make. I am only one cog in the wheel, you know. I guess I need to define exactly what my role in the school change process should be and then find ways to measure my success at those tasks. Sometimes, I feel that people attribute all school outcomes, for better or worse, to me. That isn't really fair . . . to me or to the others working in the school. In many ways, they have more control over outcomes than I do."

Lee and Marty began to identify specific activities that they saw as Lee's responsibility. First, they looked at Lee's role in facilitating and enabling processes by which the teachers and parents and students could have a real voice in the school's operations. Next, they talked about Lee's role in linking the school and community. They decided that to understand Lee's effectiveness, they needed to ask questions about specific ways Lee supported team decision making as well as how Lee clarified and supported Vibrant Spring's mission both inside and outside the school.

Marty pointed out that his observations of Lee's performance over the last year revealed that several teams (e.g., the School Planning Council, the Teacher Assistance Team, and the personnel search team) met and were making decisions in specified areas; thus Lee could be considered effective at establishing decision-making teams. Also, Lee could be considered successful at establishing opportunities for the faculty's professional growth and development because Lee regularly arranged for teachers to attend conferences and workshops. Both Lee and Marty noted that some links with the community also had been built; invited parents had begun to attend conferences and workshops with the teachers, and Lee was a regular at community group meetings like the Rotary Club. Still, Lee doubted that everyone in the community, especially those without children in the school, knew or understood the school's mission.

"We need to establish a process formally to assess my effectiveness in facilitating these processes. This is the kind of information we need—the board and I—to answer that question about how I am doing as principal. I already can see at least one area I need more work on!" admitted Lee.

Marty added, "We still need outcome data, but let's not focus entirely on you for these. Accountability for results should be school based." They talked about compiling a school portfolio that might include program evaluation reports, team meeting results, reports of resource allocation and use, and assessments of student goal achievement as well as student performance outcomes. "One outcome of your student advisory team that I was impressed with was that decision to charge for parking stickers and then use the funds for things like refurbishing that snack area—it's really working and nobody has complained," added Marty.

"Let's see what the school planning council can come up with for evaluating outcomes. We are looking at a lot of effort, but I think people would be willing to do it because we are hungry for that kind of feedback. Folks are working pretty hard, but we don't necessarily know what's happening. I can use the information to share the credit for success—and to enlist help where it's needed. And with solid outcome information we can show the world what we accomplish! Let's talk with the council about developing a school-based evaluation."

*   *   *

We see that Lee and the superintendent are concerned on several levels about getting useful evaluation information. We suggest that principals of dynamic schools be evaluated with a continuous and participatory process that is school based and links reflection with plans for action. Our approach looks at processes, activities, and products. It recognizes that school improvement is the result of complex environmental interactions involving the whole school community. Finally, the perspective we suggest is horizontal rather than hierarchical (Rizvi, 1990), that is, it considers a broad spectrum of evaluation usages and accountability to a variety of constituencies.

We believe that assessment should parallel the way work and tasks are organized in dynamic schools. Because the underlying philosophy of dynamic schools recognizes teamwork and school-based responsibility, evaluation must include both individual and school-based components. Thus principals-in-charge should be assessed individually regarding their leadership processes, whereas outcome measures should rely on school-based evaluation.

In this chapter, we lay the groundwork for our alternative design for evaluating the principal-in-charge of a dynamic school by reviewing past practices on administrative evaluation and outlining our view of evaluation and accountability in schools that have chosen to work toward improvement. We then detail our proposed evaluation design.

The Need for a Different System of Evaluation for School Improvement

Schools and the work of their principals are being evaluated informally every day. Parents pass judgment as their children report each day's events; real estate agents rate the schools in each community for potential buyers; local businesses measure the schools on the basis of their experiences with the young people they hire. The evaluation of the principal is tightly linked to the evaluation of the school. The school has little control over these types of informal evaluations, which are mostly summative. A more formalized school-based evaluation design would give people who care about improving their school and its public image some tools to control judgments of effectiveness and to fulfill the other crucial roles of evaluation.

An accountability system for schools is used to ensure that teachers and administrators are doing their jobs to provide quality education and that they are using appropriated funds as policy dictates. The purpose of evaluation includes, but goes beyond, accountability. Evaluation looks at programs and personnel and seeks to discover *why* the programs have had the determined effect and *whether* the determined effect is the one that the school community wants. The cycle of evaluation, which includes assessment, planning and design, implementation, and evaluation, can serve as a key strategy in program and personnel improvement.

One of the most important targets and clients of evaluation is the principal-in-charge, because leadership and evaluation are tightly linked. Leadership shapes events, and evaluation can change the shape of those events (Glasman, 1986). The ability to lead depends, in part, on the leader's ability to understand his or her own desires and those of the members of the organization and to translate these desires into actions that produce a desired shape of events (Glasman, 1986). Evaluation information, then, helps the principal understand desires and shape events, just as it shapes people's beliefs about the school and its leader. In sum, evaluation is a key strategy for school improvement.

Traditional approaches to administrative evaluation have fallen short in providing useful information to principals and others for the type of school improvement efforts taking place in dynamic schools. The approach we propose below differs substantively and procedurally from existing and traditional approaches to administrative evaluation. Traditional principal evaluation is informal and focused almost entirely on process: Is the building functioning smoothly? Does the principal operate within the allocated budget? Is the principal liked by the parents? Does the community appear satisfied? Data like attendance figures have been the primary product measures. In other words, principals have traditionally been evaluated on their ability to keep the ship afloat and to prevent anything or anybody from rocking the boat.

These images of administrative evaluation are grounded in shared myths and common sense understandings of practice, because reliable information on past administrator evaluation is not readily available. Documentation of practices used by districts to evaluate principals is sketchy; moreover, a preliminary review yields no noteworthy synthesis of empirical and conceptual literature related to evaluation of administrative practice.

This type of traditional evaluation is also reported as common practice from many principals. The total sample of principals who participated in the *High School and Beyond* (USDE, 1984) survey responded to a general question about their performance evaluation. Specifically, the principals were asked, "On a scale of one to six, how much influence do you feel each of the following has upon how your performance as evaluated by *your superiors?*" The results of the responses to this question are reported in Table 6.1. The means indicate that these principals believe that the most important influence on their evaluation by their superiors is running an efficiently administered school. Second in importance is having a good disciplinary environment in the school. Third is parent and community reactions to the school, and last is the performance of the school's students on standardized tests or in gaining admission to college.

The ranking of these issues suggests that these secondary school principals largely believe that they are favorably evaluated by keeping an orderly, tight ship, both in terms of the students (disciplinary environment) and in regard to their teachers and other staff (having efficient administration).

The principals indicate that parental and community reactions, such as academic achievement and college admission, have relatively little impact on their performance appraisal. They sense, perhaps, that they will receive a favorable performance evaluation from their superintendents if they do not make waves or rock the boat. These findings seem a far cry from the types of answers we would expect from principals in dynamic schools for which community input and accountability are central forces.

Table 6.1 Principals' Reports of the Influence of Various Factors on How Their Performance Is Evaluated by Their Superiors[a]

Factor	Mean[b]	Standard Deviation
Efficient administration	5.14	0.93
Good disciplinary environment	5.02	0.97
Parent or community reaction	4.80	1.08
Student performance on standardized tests or college admission	3.39	1.47

NOTES: [a]Based on public school principals' responses to the administrator survey of *High School and Beyond* (USDE, 1984); $N = 358$.
[b]Range = 1 to 6.

More recently, the recognition of the principal as an important component in an effective school (Andrews & Soder, 1987; Bossert, Dwyer, Rowan, & Lee, 1982; Edmonds & Fredericksen, 1987; Hallinger & Murphy, 1987) has opened discussion of principal evaluation. The connection in this literature between strong principal leadership behavior and student achievement introduced notions about school outcome-based evaluation for the principal. Restructuring efforts that have focused on principals have linked principals' performance assessments to schools' outcomes (Cibulka, 1989) and have suggested holding the principals accountable for student achievement (National Governors' Association, 1990). Even the public overwhelmingly favors rewarding principals based on their schools' success (Elam, 1990).

Career ladder programs for principals are another evaluation method designed to reward school administrators for measurable school improvement. The South Carolina Principal Incentive Program (PIP), for example, emphasizes student achievement gains in determining principals who will receive incentive awards (MGT of America, 1990). The Tennessee Career Ladder Administrator/Supervisor System uses a more complex system to determine merit pay recipients (Tennessee State Board of Education, 1990) but increases depend on a final score. A team of raters draws this score from identified domains of competence, which include outcome data. In these and other evaluation systems, the principal is held accountable for results of organizational activities.

Several states, like Illinois, have legislated new criteria for certification and reward of principals, but there is a dearth of empirical evidence to justify connecting legislated requirements to actual principal performance and school improvement. In fact, research reveals no clear relationship between the attributes of school principals and levels of student achievement (Deal, 1987; Glasman, 1986; Lee, 1987), and the link between principal behavior and school outcomes is, at best, indirect (Boyan, 1988; Heck, Larsen, & Marcoulides, 1990). In sum, while most constituencies today recognize the importance of the principal, few evaluation practices have successfully assessed this complex role. Currently, the overwhelming majority of districts in the United States use summative findings by a sole evaluator-supervisor as the only source of input in administrator evaluations (Educational Research Service, 1985).

Evaluation in a Dynamic School

We suggest that principals-in-charge of dynamic schools have new and different roles that require a novel approach to evaluation. Principals-in-charge are directly responsible for process and indirectly responsible for product. Thus a realistic evaluation for this principal must include an individual accountability for enabling the processes of a dynamic school as well as a school-based accountability for products. In this evaluation, leadership processes will be individually assessed, and outcome assessments will be school-based (Figure 6.1). Our proposed evaluation emphasizes internal as well as external accountability. Consequently, we suggest the establishment of a school-based team to coordinate and support the evaluation activities.

Our view of evaluation aims to establish an inquiry ethic and a commitment to collective problem solving that would permeate the school (Darling-Hammond & Snyder, 1992). We see mechanisms for review of practices by teachers, principals, and students

Targets of Evaluation

Uses of Evaluation	Principal	School
Informative	process	process
Formative	process	process and product
Summative	process	product

Figure 6.1. School-based accountability in dynamic schools.
NOTE: All evaluation is conducted by the school evaluation team.

established as regularized evaluation activities. These activities create opportunities for using assessment data and other feedback to inform decision making at all levels of evaluation use. Some activities focus on process, and others focus on product. Because of the pervasiveness of these activities, a schoolwide team must be assigned the responsibility of coordinating evaluation.

The team's efforts promote *horizontal accountability* that emphasizes accountability to the entire school community, that is, to all constituents within the school environment—principal, teachers, parents, and students—rather than to the hierarchy of the bureaucracy (Rizvi, 1990). The client then, is not just the school board or the state, but all those individuals who are involved in program development, implementation, and use. Horizontal accountability supports the inquiry ethic of the school by recognizing everyone's responsibility for success and by providing opportunity for reflection.

Traditionally, evaluation is seen as playing two roles (Scriven, 1967). Summative evaluation offers a final determination of the worth of a program or individual's performance in a role. It is not designed to be constructive; rather it is designed to be ultimately judgmental and primarily used by those stakeholders who will make some decision about program or individual continuation. Formative evaluation, on the other hand, is conceptualized as constructive. In both roles, evaluation serves to inform decision making.

We see another crucial role for evaluation in the dynamic school environment: Evaluation must be informative. Unlike formative data, which are used to shape the program, informative data simply help build an accumulated pool of knowledge about the program. At early stages of program implementation or of a person's performance in a position, evaluation data are useful to inform program personnel or individuals about what is happening. Although data collection and analysis are in too early a stage to interpret with any conclusive meaning, display of data can simply inform the practitioner and decision makers in a variety of ways. For example, in the CAP evaluation, we reviewed early analyses of the Case Status Record Keeper with the program planners, team members, and the state board of education. We offered no interpretations for the data and made no attempt to assign meaning to emergent patterns. This feedback served to legitimate the program and laid a groundwork for a deeper understanding of the program than would have been possible had we waited for formative interpretations or summative results. Through the use of informative evaluation, stakeholders become an active part of the inquiry process.

As mentioned, the responsibility for evaluation in the dynamic school rests with an evaluation team. The team's work is comprehensive in nature. First, the team looks at the specific roles of the principal: the facilitator, the balancer, and the flag bearer/bridger. Why does the team focus on these roles? It is through these roles that the principal enables other adults to assume leadership within the school, carries the message of the school into the community, and coordinates the internal and external worlds. The principal of a dynamic school manipulates these school process variables. It is the working of these process variables that results in school outcomes.

We know that some of the principal's leadership activities (e.g., the amount of time spent directly observing classroom practices, promoting discussion about instructional issues, and emphasizing student assessment for program improvement) appear to be good predictors of school performance (Heck, 1992). The evaluation team also works with the principal to design measures for these activities and to create opportunities for reflection about their impact.

Next, the team looks at school outcomes, or products. These include measures of effects from policies, programming, and allocation of resources. These are products of the total school environment for which principals are only indirectly responsible, because they facilitate the processes through which the outcomes are produced. Again, the evaluation coordinating team assembles data on outcomes and creates opportunities through which appropriate stakeholders may reflect on and use the information.

Because process and product surface as mutual components of leadership, they are mutual components of evaluation. Product, or outcomes, are the result of process. But products, in turn, impact the process. Process is shaped largely by what people believe, and the results of the process then serve to alter what people believe. As a result, information about both the product and the process shape beliefs, or judgments. Specifically, school outcomes themselves cause educators to rethink their beliefs and practices (Wick, 1987), thus influencing the process and, indirectly, the leadership actions of a principal. Information used to evaluate (informatively, formatively, and summatively) the work of the principal in enabling the processes and the work of the members of the organization in executing the processes into product is part of the change process in a dynamic school. Thus a useful evaluation will not use a linear cause-and-effect design.

The evaluation we are suggesting is anything but linear. Rather, it recognizes the complexity of the principal's work. Of this work, instructional leadership—which the literature regularly associates with the most common evaluation criteria: student achievement—is only one key element in the dynamic school's social and environmental milieus. All the elements contribute to determining student achievement (Heck, 1992), so we propose an evaluation that considers contributions of multiple individual and organizational elements. In this evaluation, leadership processes will be individually assessed, and outcome assessment will be school based (see Figure 6.1).

Finally, this type of evaluation serves several clients, both internal and external to the school. We see a top priority for this evaluation as being a catalyst for ongoing school improvement, so the first clients are the school faculty and principal themselves. Next, the superintendent and the school board need this evaluative view of the principal and the school to inform their decision making. Parents need the information to understand and support the operation of their children's place of learning. Similarly, community groups and businesses can use the information to define and proclaim a community asset and to choose aspects of the school program to support. In sum, our proposed evaluation can yield information for many stakeholders.

In the next two sections of this chapter we present in more detail the two crucial aspects of evaluation in the dynamic school: assessing principal's leadership processes and assessing school outcomes.

Assessing the Principal's Leadership Processes

A useful evaluation of principals of dynamic schools looks at those activities for which they are directly responsible, that is, establishing and supporting team decision making, manipulating resources, articulating the school's mission and engaging with the external environment. Specific questions that the team needs to address include the following:

- Do people, both inside and outside the school, understand what we are trying to do (our mission)?
- Is teacher leadership emerging?
- What decision-making bodies have been established in the school? Do they meet? How often? Are they making decisions? What decisions are they making? How do people feel about these meetings and decisions?

- What opportunities for growth and development have been established? Do people take advantage of these opportunities? How do people feel about their participation?
- What links with the community have been established? Are school environment relations tended to?
- What resources have been created or tapped? How have these resources been manipulated?

Answers to these questions yield a rich source of evidence on which to understand the work of the principal. The team members and the principal review and reflect on these data. Because the evaluation teams are school based, each team develops a plan to use the data for meeting its specific needs. All three levels of use, informative, formative, and summative, are considered.

The teams are reviewing principals' activities and behaviors that directly affect school processes and that would then, in turn, affect school outcomes. In other words, the teams collect evidence that indicates whether the principals are enabling the teams to function and whether these functions would change the outcomes for children in the school. Reviewing these data can make it clear whether the principal is essential to the success of the school.

Principals-in-charge take many actions that can be identified as directly supporting the processes important to a dynamic school. Noticing and analyzing these actions contribute one set of data for evaluating a principal-in-charge. Although the task of assessing the principal's performance in facilitating, balancing, and bridging falls to the school evaluation team, the principal's contribution is critical to the team's work. The principal-in-charge models the inquiry ethic that is the basis of the evaluation process. As a reflective practitioner (Schon, 1983) the principal-in-charge examines his or her practice and its impact on the school's practice. Moreover, as the formal leader of the organization, the principal is ultimately accountable, and thus responsible, for his or her own evaluation. The principal-in-charge is the driving force behind the evaluation team.

Assessing School Outcomes

The second set of data for evaluating the principal must be school outcomes. But the principal is not directly responsible for these outcomes. Rather, the outcomes are products of processes—the results of group interactions and team processes occurring in the school environment, an environment that the principal as leader has been instrumental in establishing. Thus the outcome measures, although still a component of the principal's evaluation, are school based. That is, school outcomes must consider the total school context.

Considering the school context means that more than student achievement outcomes must be examined. For outcome assessment, the evaluation team must ask questions such as:

- What programs have school-based management teams created? How are these programs operating?
- What solutions for school problems have teams found and implemented? How are these solutions working?
- What community relations programs or activities have been implemented? What is their rate of success?
- Have school decision teams sought and allocated resources? In what ways and with what results?
- Have teams created new policies? What effect have the policies had on school operation?
- What are students learning?

Answers to these questions should come from a variety of data sources: program evaluation reports, team meeting records, systematic observations of planned events, budget or audit reports, student performance assessments, and student achievement scores. An example of the documentation to be included in the portfolio might be reports from the team, which uses a descriptive review process to assess the status and progress of individual children (as described by Carini, 1986, and as used by New York's Brooklyn New

School, Darling-Hammond & Snyder, 1992). These data can be compiled into school portfolios by the evaluation-coordinating team. We suggest that the outcome assessment be treated as an ongoing activity to which all members of the school community contribute, rather than one performed by an individual in a supervisory position. This activity is coordinated by the evaluation team. If school community stakeholders assume ownership for this aspect of the evaluation, the experience becomes both informative, in that they create knowledge about their work, and formative, in that they use this knowledge to improve their work. Members examine each other's work, understand and determine its effectiveness, and explore alternative strategies for improving their environment.

The use of outcome data is illustrated by the CAP evaluation. We compiled computer-analyzed team records that told us the types of problems for which teachers referred students, the length of meetings, the proposed interventions, the success of the proposed interventions, and the number and success of follow-up meetings. Team members and policymakers found this information useful in understanding the learning problems commonly dealt with in schools and in developing the programs to address these problems.

We also collected numbers of students identified as learning disabled over the first 5 years of program implementation. Although we could not directly attribute any changes in identification to team effects, this summative information did reveal any increases or decreases that occurred during this time. That identifications plateaued and began to decrease coincidentally with the establishment of teams gave us reason to look closely at what role the program may have played and how this role could be developed. Similarly, while student achievement score increases cannot be directly attributed to the actions and behaviors of the principal, that student scores in effective schools tend to be higher causes researchers to look closely at characteristics of principals in these schools and to propose strategies for strengthening these characteristics.

A feasible design for conducting the outcome assessment involves compiling a school portfolio containing the kind of rich outcome data from the sources we have suggested above. (Portfolios are already widely used for teacher and student assessment; see Schulman, 1988; Wolf, 1991). Evaluation team members represent the various constituencies that contribute to school success: teachers from different programs and activities in operation, parents and possibly other community representatives, the principal, and possibly a student (depending on the age range of the student body). In a dynamic school, a body that already exists, such as the planning team, will design an appropriate composition and task definition to meet the needs of the school.

The school portfolio can produce a summative evaluation with solid, defensible data to document the school's record of accomplishment. The team can also analyze these results by matching them with the established mission and philosophy of the school to produce a formative evaluation. Reviewing the outcomes, the team can form a picture of the school and ask the following:

- What kind of school are we? Are we pleased with this picture?
- What kind of work do we do and what kind of learning occurs? Again, are we pleased with this picture?
- What forces, individuals, or groups are contributing to or responsible for the picture?
- What kind of changes are occurring in this school? Are they changes that improve the school environment?
- Are we moving in the direction we want?
- What forces, individuals, groups are contributing to or responsible for these changes?
- How can we reinforce the positive aspects?
- What might be barriers or potential barriers to school improvement changes?
- What do we need to strengthen our processes and outcomes?

Discussion and analysis of answers to these questions can result in a formative evaluation that serves as a needs assessment, identifying areas in which to focus new improvement efforts. This team, school-based accountability approach is also important as a means to support and motivate teachers toward increased participation in team collaboration, shared decision making, and other group work efforts.

Evaluating the Evaluation Approach

The fundamental purpose of any evaluation plan, whether of persons or programs, must be to improve the provision of services to students and society (Joint Committee on Standards for Educational Evaluation, 1988). Thus we would be remiss if we did not consider the extent to which our proposed evaluation of a school leader accomplishes this purpose. To this end, the Joint Committee on Standards for Educational Evaluation (1988) offers *The Personnel Evaluation Standards* to use in assessing systems for evaluating educators. The standards are divided into four categories that correspond to four basic attributes of sound evaluation:

- *Propriety:* Does the evaluation determine if educators are effectively and ethically meeting the needs of students?
- *Utility:* Is the evaluation informative, timely, and influential? Does it focus on predetermined uses? Is it conducted by persons with expertise and credibility?
- *Feasibility:* Is the evaluation efficient, easy to use, and viable in the face of social, political, and legal forces and constraints? Will it be adequately funded?
- *Accuracy:* Will it produce sound, trustworthy information?

The principal-in-charge aims to build a school in which all students are comfortable, so that they may learn to the best of their abilities. Our ultimate purpose in proposing this alternative evaluation approach is to provide a more accurate and realistic picture of the principal's success in achieving this goal. Therefore, we believe that our approach, because it draws from a variety of data sources to examine both individual and organizational effects, does meet the propriety standard; our holistic evaluation does probe the questions of whether the principal and school are fulfilling the institutional mission and of whether that mission is educationally sound.

Because the principal and internal teams have a great deal of control over the conduct of the evaluation and because a primary use of the evaluation is to be informative and formative to these players themselves, we see our approach as meeting the utility standard. Because an informative, timely, influential, and relevant evaluation with appropriate follow-up is in the best interests of the members of the dynamic school, placing the onus of this standard on their shoulders does not seem unreasonable.

As our evaluation approach is to be collaboratively developed and monitored and draws from already existing data sources, it is feasible. The major resource required will be the time and energy of school-based evaluation teams. That this approach to accountability fosters internal and professional, rather than external or bureaucratic control, assists in generating the necessary time and energy (see Darling-Hammond & Berry, 1988, and Darling-Hammond & Snyder, 1992, for the definition of professional versus bureaucratic control used here). In other words, this model, which views teachers as capable of making complex educational decisions on behalf of diverse students, is self-rewarding.

Meeting the accuracy standard depends, in part, on the accuracy of those data already collected for other purposes. For example, the program evaluations and the student testing data to be included in the portfolios must themselves be technically accurate and valid. We admonish all school-based evaluation teams and principals systematically and completely to document all procedures that the team uses. Also, the team's work should be reviewed regularly by an external source so that problems are surfaced and revisions are made.

Summary

School-based outcomes assessment, combined with individual process assessment of principals produces a more holistic picture on which to evaluate the performance of principals of dynamic schools than one based entirely on outcome data. This holistic picture can benefit principals by enabling them to see and understand what they are doing and, in formative ways, reveal strengths and weaknesses. The picture can also inform superintendents so that they may better know how to support or critique the work of their principals. School boards and other policy-making bodies may use the picture as a summative display of the achievements of the school and its principal.

Our holistic evaluation perspective is appropriate for a dynamic school with reflective practitioners who are driven by an inquiry ethic. As always, the role of the principal-in-charge in establishing this ethic is crucial. The principal encourages, models, and legitimizes the inquiry process. The principals-in-charge are inquirers, ensuring that their own effectiveness as facilitators, balancers, and bridgers is examined and ensuring that whole school processes are examined.

Still, developing an evaluation-minded school (see Nevo, 1991) through establishing the school evaluation system that we propose is a complex process requiring long-term commitment. Although we offer a framework to assess both individual leadership processes and school outcomes, others have more completely and adequately described the principles underlying training needs and recommended strategies for implementing such an evaluation system (see, e.g., Glasman & Nevo, 1988; Nevo, 1991). One caveat noted by Nevo (1991) that we underscore is the need to institutionalize the evaluation-coordinating team as a permanent component in the structure of the school. Because this team is responsible for coordinating the principal's evaluation, the team's operations, unlike other teams in the school, should not depend primarily on the principal's facilitation to flourish. Although still school based and school defined, the team and its task description should be officially recognized and legitimized by the board and superintendent. These bodies should provide for training, technical assistance, and reward for team members. In other words, the team needs both internal and external validation.

The approach for evaluating the principal of a dynamic school becomes more than a means to assess an individual's productivity. Instead, the evaluation becomes a key strategy in the total change process of the school. Evaluation of the principal of a dynamic school takes on a new role; evaluation becomes one of the continuous, participatory processes that is integral to the school's reflection of and growth for improvement.

The Learner

Preparing Leaders of Dynamic Schools

Principals-in-charge respond differently to the forces impacting schools than do their traditional counterparts. They have different orientations, or ways of interpreting their worlds, that influence their leadership behaviors. How can teachers or other functioning principals become leaders of dynamic schools? This chapter examines the knowledge, skills, and experiences helpful for preparing and shaping future principals-in-charge.

Janet and Tony had lingered for another cup of coffee with Lee after the teacher assistance team meeting. Lee knew they wanted to talk about something. "So what's on your minds?"

Janet began: "We know that, starting next year, several of the district schools will have openings for principals. Both Tony and I have been thinking about making a formal move into administration—we see ourselves as teacher-leaders. We've been involved in much of the decision making at Vibrant Springs through the different teams, but we think that now we are ready to use some of our skills in the role of principal."

"But," Tony continued, "we'd like your advice on how best to be prepared. I already have principal certification; Janet has a master's degree but not in school administration. She has been a department chair, and we have both led at least one team at

Vibrant Springs. In neither case, we realize, does that mean we are prepared to be the kind of principal you are."

"And that is the point," interrupted Janet. "We don't just want to be principals, like the one I had in the school where I worked before I came to Vibrant Springs. We want to be principals who are able to lead the kind of school we have here—a school where all of us, teachers, students, parents, feel we have a voice in what happens. We need to learn to be principals who can take a stand without shoving it down people's throats!"

Lee responded, "Well, I think you have raised three issues: What do you need to meet formal requirements? What do you need based on your individual professional experiences? And what do you need to be a principal who facilitates and connects as well as manages? The first one is easy to answer; you find out what is required for certification.

"The next two are not as simple. You, like others who will be seeking the positions, bring different experiences. In my mind, you two have an important advantage—you have not only held teacher-leader positions, but you have worked in a school that is not managed top-down, a school where, as you already mentioned, many voices are heard in its decision-making processes. You need a preparation program that capitalizes on your rich experiences and fills in areas of knowledge and skill you do not have."

"That's right. I certainly do not need more instruction on, or experience in, instructional leadership, but I am a blank page on budget and finances," agreed Tony.

"That goes for me too," added Jane. "But, that third issue, becoming the kind of principal who leads a school like Vibrant Springs, takes a kind of attitude, a way of looking at the running of a school. A really good preparation program will offer something to help get at that, too. But what?"

"Principals who are already managing traditional schools might learn how to transform their schools into ones more like ours if they participated in the kind of preparation we are talking about now. So the question expands beyond what into how can it reach a wide audience. It might not be a traditional degree program," Lee concluded.

As the others rose to leave, Lee made some notes to call the regional lab and service center to see what might be available for Janet and Tony. Lee also picked up the phone to call Marty to talk about these very issues of preparing teachers with leadership experiences for principalships and of transforming other practicing principals.

* * *

Vibrant Springs School's district, like many districts across the United States, has several vacancies for school leadership positions for the next school year. Research indicates that as many as half of all elementary and middle school principals will retire within the next decade (National Association of Elementary School Principals, 1992). Furthermore, as many as 70% of all school administrators will enter retirement within the next 10 years (Poston, 1992). Some of these vacancies will be filled by teacher-leaders, others will be filled by classroom teachers, while still others will be filled by practicing principals moving from one school to another. What type of development can principals receive to be leaders of dynamic schools? How can these new principals be leaders that shape dynamic schools?

The objective of this chapter is to stimulate discussion about preparing and developing leadership that is oriented to the new roles of principals-in-charge: facilitating the internal school, balancing within the hierarchy, coordinating the external environment, and monitoring the evaluation-minded school. If principals are to be in charge, they require different preparation programs and alternative development modes that go beyond certification requirements. In this chapter, we discuss such programs. We briefly review the rationale of present preparation programs to understand the changes that are necessary both to prepare principals for their new roles and to enable them to maintain their momentum of continuous development. We discuss program design and orientations as illustrations of the types of approaches that can be implemented to prepare leaders of dynamic schools (Figure 7.1). At the end of this discussion, we present the development experiences of some principals of dynamic schools.

Our purpose is not to review educational administration training programs. Scholars have comprehensively reviewed leadership preparation approaches (Hallinger, 1992; Jacobson & Conway, 1990; Murphy, 1993), and numerous national commissions have addressed problems facing the field of educational administration and posed solutions, many of which include changes in training programs (i.e., National Commission on Excellence in Educational Administration and National Policy Board for Educational Administration). Our interest is in contributing to the ongoing discussion about leadership development.

Furthermore, we do not believe that leadership can be shaped in a linear fashion. Clearly, leadership training does not automatically lead to more effective principals who, in turn, lead to more successful schools. This linear path has been followed in response to the effective schools movement (Murphy, 1993). Consequently, many programs continue to try to develop those specific traits among principals who have been identified as highly successful (Barth, 1986). In contrast, we suggest a revolving door approach to leadership development in which both aspiring and practicing principals continually participate, entering and exiting, in various development activities.

Leadership Development for Principals of Dynamic Schools

In the 1980s there were numerous calls for the redesign of educational administration preparation programs (NCEE, 1987). The design of the new type of training to be required for school leaders was heavily influenced by school improvement research that indicated that effective schools had principals who provided strong instructional leadership, facilitated norms of teacher collegiality, and provided a clear vision of school goals. Hence, training

---

Program Design

• needs based • criteria based • inquiry based • skill development

Leadership Orientations

- facilitating the internal leadership of schools
- working within the hierarchy
- optimizing the external management of schools
- leading the evaluation-minded school
- understanding the social context of education

Figure 7.1. Essential Components of Leadership Development

programs were criticized for emphasizing building management (e.g., finance, law) rather than instructional leadership, curriculum development, and student evaluation (Fallon, 1979; Pellicer, 1982; Peterson & Finn, 1985). Support for the need for this type of training was found in a survey among 337 principals throughout the United States who rated instructional leadership expectations as the area where training is most needed (Snyder & Johnson, 1985). Murphy (1993) suggests that heightened interest in increasing the teaching and learning components of preparation programs is based on empirical research that indicates that effective schools are characterized by administrators who emphasize pedagogical matters.

Our analysis indicates that preparation programs designed in the 1980s for developing instructional and pedagogical leadership skills may not be sufficient when training principals to be in charge of dynamic schools. Rallis (1986), for instance, maintains that instructional leadership, to be effective, must come from the teaching ranks, whereas principals must be concerned with managing the school. Looking at the needs of principals in dynamic schools, we see that they go beyond pedagogy.

Our view of leadership development for principals-in-charge of dynamic schools is based on the notion of lifelong learning. Principals of dynamic schools accept responsibility for their ongoing professional renewal and development. As Wimpleberg (1990) suggests, we replace *learning place* for *workplace* in McGregor's Theory Y, and thus assume that principals "carry an internal quest to become better at their trade, that they want to learn how to improve the contributions they can make to the schools and school districts where they work, and that they want involvement in their professional development" (Wimpleberg, 1990, p. 107). Recent evaluations of different types of leadership development programs have suggested that programs are moderately successful at developing a personally grounded belief in the importance of lifelong learning (Hallinger, 1992, p. 310).

When we speak of preparation, we are referring to a wide variety of socialization experiences, both formal and informal, both pre-service and in-service. Hence, we rely on Greenfield's (1987) framework for continuous development for school leaders. Specifically, Greenfield (1987) outlines "processes and conditions that mediate the acquisition of knowledge, skills, beliefs and personal dispositions required to perform a given role satisfactorily" (p. 65). The socialization processes that contribute to leadership development are both formal and informal and the content is both technical and moral.

Formal socialization processes, or formal leadership development, refers to specific learning situations in which both the role of the participant and the content of the program are clearly specified in advance. The role of the participant is explicitly defined as learner. These types of formal processes include degree-granting programs, staff development, and in-service activities.

In contrast, informal processes refer to those situations in which the role of the learner and the material to be covered are not defined. These natural learning and development situations occur informally as one discovers and learns norms, traits, attitudes, and orientations in a given job setting, or in moving from one position to another. For example, Greenfield (1985) found that teachers aspiring to administration take on more of the values and orientations of the administrative group and interact more frequently with administrators. These informal experiences present many opportunities for development and preparation of teachers for new future administrative roles.

Greenfield (1987) suggests that both technical and moral content can be gained through formal and informal processes. Technical content refers to specific knowledge and skills required to fulfill a role, and moral content refers to sentiments, beliefs, and orientations of the role incumbents. Leaders of dynamic schools need development in both of these content areas.

In this chapter we discuss leadership development over an expanded period of time, encompassing formal and informal processes that afford both technical and moral competencies. The goal of leadership development for principals-in-charge is to provide socialization experiences that lead to a personal leadership framework with innovative orientations (Crow, Mecklowitz, & Weekes, 1992). The concept of *principals as learners* is fundamental to the development of principals of dynamic schools (Barth, 1986). Principals of dynamic schools take individual responsibility for development.

Program Design

Principals are generally chosen from three populations of educators: classroom teachers, teacher-leaders, and administrators (e.g., vice principals and experienced principals from another school). Candidates from each population have different socialization experiences. For example, teachers who seek authority and influence beyond the classroom traditionally look toward the principalship (Peterson & Finn, 1985). These prospective leaders have been socialized and enculturated into administration from their experiences as teachers. Consequently, traditional educational administration preparation programs rely on a rather standard view of the socialization processes of prospective administrators as classroom teachers. These candidates typically come to preservice programs from the classroom with a wealth of expertise in teaching but with little experience and knowledge about the larger organizational context. At best, some of these teachers have limited management experiences in part-time leadership positions as department heads.

In contrast to this first group of prospective principals, regular classroom teachers, teacher-leaders, and experienced administrators have had varied experiences before entering the principalship. For example, empowered teacher-leaders in dynamic schools have widely varying experiences, many of which are outside of the classroom and require them to function in the larger organizational context. In fact, many of the roles and responsibilities of empowered teachers are largely congruent with functions typically carried out by administrators. These empowered teachers pass through different socialization and enculturation processes from their counterparts in traditional schools.

Empowered teachers, or teacher-leaders, bring these diverse experiences to educational leadership training programs as they prepare to be principals-in-charge. Many candidates for the principalship have had on-the-job training and experiences commensurate with the roles of the traditional principal. Training programs of the future must reflect these changes in the characteristics of the candidates (Goldring & Chen, in press). Assessment centers are helpful in providing assistance in assessing prospective school administrators. Participation in the assessment center is recommended because of the need for objective data regarding potential principals (Richardson, 1988). A major implication of the presence of varied roles and experiences among prospective principals and potential leaders is that their training and development must be needs based, criteria based, and inquiry based.

Needs Based. Leadership development opportunities must be offered in an unstandardized manner that is based on the needs of potential leaders. Not all students entering a program will need to develop and learn all the same skills and content areas, because the roles and experiences of empowered teachers in dynamic schools will most likely vary from site to site and be very different from classroom teachers or principals from traditional schools. Programs should have the flexibility to present opportunities for learning and growth according to the needs of the candidates, as they define them.

As Greenfield's (1985) framework describes, some candidates may have been formally socialized, gaining skills and knowledge through participation in a formal degree-granting educational administration program. Hence, these candidates may need exposure to the norms, attitudes, and orientations of dynamic schools through both formal and informal processes more than do potential leaders who are teacher-leaders in dynamic schools. The candidates from dynamic schools already have widespread exposure to the norms and orientations of leadership in the dynamic school but lack formal exposure to skills, knowledge, and theory.

In their recent review of administrative development programs, Hallinger and Wimpleberg (1991) note a wide range of frameworks for participants in the development of training programs. These range from no role in governance and no input in articulating program goals to a strong governance role and even individually developing goals and programs. Students in formal programs need to have some mechanism whereby their needs can be communicated to the instructors when program decisions are being made. Learner involvement is a fundamental premise of adult learning theory (Levine, 1989). Most principals' centers and institutes do involve principals in decisions regarding program content (Wimpleberg, 1990).

Criteria Based. The second point about leadership development programs for principals of dynamic schools is that they should be criteria based. Potential leaders should demonstrate they have fulfilled program criteria through both formal and informal socialization processes, through job experience, or through previous training. Murphy (1990b) refers to this as an outcome-based approach to training. Specifically, different students (and groups of students) will demonstrate mastery at different times depending on the order in which they tackle issues, the paths they select (with professional guidance) to reach an outcome, and the capacity they bring and the amount of effort they devote to the endeavor (Murphy, 1990b, p. 10).

One such program is the principal certification program at Indiana University of Pennsylvania (Erlandson & Witters-Churchill, 1990). In this program, potential leaders are evaluated along six performance areas. A highly individualized program is designed for each student based on the evaluations of the performance areas and the student's credentials. As students move through the program of workshops, seminars, and fieldwork they reach competency in each performance area.

Inquiry Based. The third issue of program design is that it should be inquiry based. In referring to inquiry-based programs, we suggest that students should be involved in the "process of discovering and distributing knowledge rather than assigning them to a passive role as consumers of the final scientific product" (Garrison, 1988, p. 488). Our programs need to orient students to the procedures of inquiry and knowledge gathering. Tom (1985) elaborates on this model of inquiry-based teacher education, describing programs that aim to promote an ongoing dialogue about actual experiences to encourage questioning of assumptions and practices. Problem-based learning is another approach with a similar goal of encouraging the practitioner to reflect on problems of practice through case studies (Bridges, 1992). The model of teacher-researcher has been set forth as a way to promote teacher inquiry, but less emphasis has been put on the role of principal-researcher.

Skill Development. In addition to these specific design issues, prospective leaders as lifelong learners should focus on developing specific skills that can enhance their roles as learners: engaging in reflective learning, applying multiple perspectives, and promoting the empowerment process.

The strong assumption that many potential leaders have on-the-job learning needs to be validated. An important skill all principals need to practice and develop, however, is learning from experience (Peterson, 1985), or reflective learning. According to Kolb (1983), this process occurs in four distinct steps: (1) concrete experience, (2) reflective analysis, (3) abstract conceptualization, and (4) active experimentation. Barth (1986) refers to a four-step reflective process: (1) reflect on practice, (2) articulate practice, (3) better understand practice, and (4) improve practice. Prestine and LeGrand (1991) describe the reflective practice in stages. The first involves focusing observations and the second consists of gaining access to and controlling individual and personal problem-solving strategies.

Leadership development programs should help leaders master learning from their on-the-job experiences by providing models and paradigms for analyzing their own activities, looking for patterns in their work, and developing sense-making skills (see Peterson, 1985). It is crucial to systematize these skills for educational leaders as they are often swept up in the moment of their actions without scrutinizing and questioning. Case records are valuable tools that can help establish reflective learning (Silver, 1987).

Special attention should be given to the issue of professional identity through the reflective process. As these candidates move toward manager-leadership positions, they should be encouraged to explore the meanings of leaving their former professional reference group. Reflective learning applied to this transition stimulates thought as to how experiences in the teaching ranks may be used to optimize leadership.

Another skill area in which principals need training is in developing the ability to apply multiple perspectives or frameworks to situations (Bolman & Deal, 1991). They should be able to analyze an organization and organizational events from a variety of models. This skill involves both learning and practice. They must learn distinct conceptual and theoretical models and practice by analyzing specific organizational incidents. The goal of applying multiple perspectives is to help principals interpret organizational phenomena, moving leaders away from merely applying specific skills to developing skills that afford a deeper understanding of organizational events (Wimpleberg, 1990). "Managers who master the ability to reframe, report a liberating sense of choice and power. They are able to develop new alternatives and new ideas about what their organization needs" (Bolman & Deal, 1991, p. 17).

Furthermore, school leaders must be able to facilitate organizational practices that allow empowerment of others. An understanding of the antecedent conditions of powerlessness and the subsequent understanding of practices that can lead to empowerment should be among the important skills of new principals. Conger and Kanungo (1988), in their comprehensive discussion of empowerment, address these two issues. A thorough understanding of the empowerment process requires analyses into the motivators at work that help bring about empowerment as well as specific strategies that may lead to empowerment such as participative management, job design, and job enlargement.

The ability to engage in reflective learning, to apply multiple perspectives to situations, and to understand thoroughly the empowerment process encourages potential leaders as learners to relate differently to their environment and experiences. Consequently, mastery of such processes facilitates their ability to create and nurture a more enabling environment in their schools.

Articulating Orientations

A crucial aspect of leadership development for principals of dynamic schools is their ability to articulate their own view of leadership or to develop a personal leadership framework. "The development of such a framework must provide potential leaders with an overarching perspective of their own organizational role and also help them to organize and make sense of the many facets of that role" (Roberts, 1990). These personal leadership frameworks should be rooted in conceptions of teaching and learning, rather than existing structures of formally defined educational leadership positions (Elmore, 1990). Potential leaders should develop their own paradigm of schooling. This requires knowledge and experiences about numerous perspectives of schooling and leadership, what we refer to as orientations.

The socialization experiences for potential leaders of dynamic schools should focus on five general orientations corresponding to the critical roles of principals-in-charge: facilitating the internal leadership of schools, working within the hierarchy, optimizing the external management of schools, leading the evaluation-minded school, and understanding the social context of education. The following discussion addresses each of these areas.

Facilitating the Internal Management of the School. In Chapter 3, we made the case that principals of dynamic schools must integrate, facilitate, and coordinate the many aspects of the internal functioning of the school so that goals and visions can be realized. Studies of effective managers in the business community indicate they spend their time on two key activities: setting an agenda for their organization and building networks to implement this agenda (Kotter, 1982). Others refer to this as *vision*. Beyond having vision, principals must facilitate the implementation of such vision; in other words, they must not only be concerned with the *what* but also the *how*.

To succeed in facilitating and integrating teaching and learning processes in schools, principals must have widespread knowledge about numerous approaches to teaching and learning (Caldwell, 1990; Hallinger, Murphy, Weil, Mesa, & Mitman, 1983). Included in these areas of expertise are the capabilities for instructional leadership.

Principals of dynamic schools are not simply facilitators of instruction, attending to the content and methods of student learning, but they are also facilitators of the work of teachers. Of central importance is the leader's role in motivating teachers. A leader needs "to ensure that teachers have the resources and learning opportunities they need, and create conditions within schools that allow students and teachers to use their motivation and capabilities to be productive learners and managers" (Hawley, 1989, p. 14).

It is the principal who coordinates school tasks and creates the necessary conditions to enable teachers and students to succeed (Kelley, 1980). As Rallis (1988) reminds us, it is the principal who must see the larger school picture and keep the whole machine greased and in total working order. This skill requires important knowledge in the areas of team building, group decision making, coordination and control mechanisms, and performance appraisal.

Special attention must be given to issues of power and authority as the prospective leaders move from collegial relationships in which leadership is exercised with peers to a hierarchical position in which authority and leadership are also embedded in relationships with subordinates. These areas are the nuts and bolts of management, which will help principals administer by integrating all aspects of life inside of school.

Working Within the Hierarchy. The role of the principal-in-charge also includes mediating between the central office and his or her school, often termed middle management (Morris et al., 1984; Goldring, 1993). We discussed in Chapter 4 the challenge confronting the principal of a dynamic school to balance the need for independence with influence from the system hierarchy. Teachers seeking leadership roles are usually not aware of the complexity of the relationship between principals and their superiors; in fact, the teacher has often contributed to the tensions in this relationship by making demands in opposition to central office or state policies. Thus, to become effective principals of dynamic schools, these teachers will need a reorientation toward the hierarchy.

This reorientation requires two foci: one on formal relationships and the other on the informal relationships. First, the potential leader must be aware of the formal policy-making processes operating in the system and the state. What laws, regulations, and guidelines have been established that affect school operation? What leeway does the school administration have while operating within these established boundaries? What influence does the principal have in their establishment in the first place and in their continuation? The principal must know and understand the roles of the superintendent and other central office personnel as well as the roles of state officials in the education department.

On the informal side, the principal must develop the skills to build effective working relationships with superiors in the hierarchy. The principal has moved from the "we-they perspective" typically held by teachers concerning the administration toward an "us perspective." The principal must be skilled in collaborating to share and define goals and strategies, in exchanging information, and in buffering. The principal must learn what is an effective working relationship with the superintendent and how to build that relationship. In sum, a potential leader of a dynamic school needs reorientation to work within the hierarchy.

Managing the Environment. Many observers of the age of restructuring have indicated that principals must begin to take on a new role, that of entrepreneur (Crow, 1991; Kerchner, 1990; Slater & Doig, 1988). Although this role is most important under choice schemes, it seems to be a critical task for all principals, and those of dynamic schools do have this entrepreneur orientation. In Chapter 5 we developed the concept we are calling *environmental leadership;* Guthrie (1990) has labeled it *enterprising.* This aspect of the principal's role includes such responsibilities as defining programs and missions for the organization and explicitly explaining and publicizing this mission to external constituencies, developing and nourishing external support for the school's mission, mobilizing resources, and bridging between internal and external needs and interests.

The CASE-IMS Model developed by the National Association of Secondary School Principals (NASSP) is an example of how principals can take charge to manage the environment (Howard & Keefe, 1991; Schmitt & Doherty, 1988). CASE-IMS represents essential strategies for realizing meaningful change in school improvement while taking stock of the environment. For example, included in this improvement process is the development of a school improvement team that may consist of teachers, students, parents, and community leaders. Activities for awareness raising acquaints students, parents, teachers, and community leaders with the team's expectations. The team collects baseline data to measure the impact of the improvement efforts, followed by an assessment that uses seven different satisfaction climate instruments. The data are translated into meaningful form for use and planning during the workshops. Members are also appointed to a special task force to make school improvement intervention recommendation. Finally, an evaluation is conducted each year and complete reassessment of priorities takes place very 3 to 5 years to study the impact of the school improvement process.

CASE-IMS involves the critical roles we see as necessary for the principals-in-charge: facilitating the internal management of the school, working within the hierarchy, optimizing the external management of schools, leading the evaluation-minded school, and understanding the social context of education. The forces that have an impact on schools will require a systematic approach to school planning and improving. This data-based approach can assist in satisfying these imperatives for school improvement.

An important part of external leadership is the budget. Many reform plans indicate that schools, as autonomous units, are responsible for budget management. Although observers note there is usually not much room for discretion after salaries, supplies, and overhead are accounted for, we believe that the fiscal aspects of leadership will become paramount in dynamic schools (Guthrie, 1990).

Budgetary discretion is a form of empowerment for principals in that it allows the principal another important avenue to pursue, implement, and publicize the school's mission. When referring to financial management, we include such skills as cost-benefit analyses, resource allocation and resource management skills, and the ability to evaluate the relationship between performance indicators and resource allocation. Principals-in-charge must develop skills in all aspects of dealing with a budget as a part of external management orientation.

Caldwell (1990) maintains that managing the school with an eye to the external context is crucial for principals. Principals must be skilled in taking account of the general environment for education in the country as well as on the state and local levels when identifying needs, formulating policies, and establishing priorities. Empowered, professional teacher-leaders and classroom teachers have experience in leading many aspects of the instructional programs in a school, but as prospective principals, they must turn some of their attention to managing external relationships and ensuring the school's survival and support in the larger environmental context.

Leading the Evaluation-Minded School. In Chapter 6, we suggest that a dynamic school is an evaluation-minded school (Nevo,

1991). The principal's role in establishing this mind-set in the school is critical, so a principal-in-charge must be prepared with an evaluation orientation. This principal must be more than reflective and self-evaluative. As leader of an evaluation-minded school, he or she must encourage, coordinate, and support the operation of a team responsible for the design and implementation of evaluation strategies as well as for the utilization of results.

A leader must not only understand evaluation processes but know how to use the information that emerges from these processes. Glasman (1986) has noted that evaluation and leadership are tightly linked skills. Leadership shapes events, whereas evaluation shapes the decisions a leader makes. In an evaluation-minded school, the process of needs assessment, planning, program implementation, and evaluation of effects becomes a task involving all organizational members. Leaders must understand and believe in this process to use evaluation themselves and to enable the process to become institutionalized as a permanent component of the school structure. A leader, then, uses evaluation information, both formally and informally, to understand the status of the organization, to make choices for the benefit of the organization, and to influence organizational support for decisions.

Training for evaluation includes both developing a conceptual framework and practicing hands-on in planning and collecting, analyzing, and interpreting data, and in utilizing the data. Although principals-in-charge will not necessarily be conducting any evaluations themselves, they need both theoretical and practical background so that they may coordinate and seek resources for the teams who are responsible for evaluation. Teachers who have been working in dynamic schools will be likely to have strong theoretical and practical backgrounds because their schools are evaluation minded. But teachers and administrators from traditional schools will lack this orientation and will need extensive exposure to evaluation ideas and opportunities for practice.

Finally, supporting our revolving door metaphor of principal preparation, all principals, whether they are new in dynamic schools or are experienced principals-in-charge, will need periodic refreshing of their understanding of evaluation and its uses. Sometimes even an auditing of the principal's and the school's evaluation processes is called for. Developing an evaluation orientation, then, is a complex and ongoing process.

Grasping the Social Context of Education and Schooling. Schools, however successful, are central to our society. The link between schools and the larger society is constantly in flux, but there is the consistent expectation from schools and the community alike that schools will be attuned to the pace and tones of the world. This is not an easy task in today's complicated world, as educators are called on to deal with broken homes, racial tensions, economic hardships, and the like. This requires educational leaders to have a worldview understanding of the place of schools in society. Many preparation programs of the past have not been interested in developing the historical and social context of education. They have not considered it part of their mission to provide their students with a broadened understanding of world trends that have an impact on schools (see Murphy, 1993).

Preparation programs for dynamic schools must create a heightened sense of intellectualism and world awareness among their students by teaching more about the history, philosophy and politics of education, comparative education trends, and institutional impacts on society. This knowledge will provide leaders with a context and intellectual base to develop their paradigm of schools and a personal framework of leadership. For example, "administrators steeped in history, philosophy, and politics understand the implications of an equity agenda versus one based on meritocracy and the concomitant policies likely to emanate from the acceptance of one versus the other. They can anticipate and, therefore, plan intelligently" (Mulkeen & Tetenbaum, 1990, p. 17). Our school leaders need to have a clearer understanding about the heterogeneous needs and cultures of our populations and how this impacts on managing and leading schools.

Leadership Development Experiences
of Principals-in-Charge

In this section, we present the leadership development processes of principals-in-charge from our data sets. It is important
to note that we are not saying that these principals are principals
of dynamic schools because of their leadership development practices. Rather we illustrate how these principals are highly committed
to their own professional development, continually participating in
training activities at different points in time.

Ken's background offers a prototype of preparation for a principal-in-charge. As a high school teacher working on his master's
in curriculum, he built a relationship with an influential professor.
"I guess you could say he was a mentor. He encouraged me to
become active in a national group promoting core curriculum. I
attended several national conferences of this group, and I served
as an officer. I learned a lot about what is possible because I met
so many people who were really trying to make a specific change
in their schools," he recalls.

Upon finishing his degree, he became a vice principal in a
junior high in the system. "That was when I attended a principals'
institute at a major university. That experience really got me
thinking about being a principal and what kind of principal I
wanted to be. I didn't feel ready for the role of principal when
I got the principalship of Midway High School—it seemed like
just yesterday that I had been teaching there." Very soon, Ken
became involved in a national outcomes-based education group.
He heard Ted Sizer speak at a conference and brought back to
Midway the idea of joining the Coalition of Essential Schools.
As the leader of one of the early coalition schools, Ken has
attended conferences, led workshops, and served on a variety
of task forces. "I have begun a doctoral program, but I probably
never will find the time to finish. I know that I will always be
involved in some learning activity anyway. The only way I can
stay alive professionally is to grow. To be the kind of principal

I need to be, I need to continue to learn, but not necessarily in a formal program."

Several of the CAP and LRE principals also illustrate reliance on a varied background as well as ongoing education. Eileen has a master's in education and had been an elementary curriculum director before becoming a principal. For professional development, she regularly participates in a regional leadership academy and has attended an institute sponsored by the Association for Supervision and Curriculum Development (ASCD).

Mike has a master's degree in educational administration and was a director of special education for the system before he became principal. "My experience in a district-level position, one that also gave me a lot of contact with parents, has really given me a special preparation to be a principal. A lot of people want to go the other way, you know, from a building-level position to the central office, but I am glad I did it this way. I have a much broader view," he explains.

Marsha's rich background as a principal first of a rural school and then of an international school in the Pacific has offered her a unique preparation to become the principal-in-charge of the dynamic school she now leads. "I think I have seen everything," she comments. "In both of those other schools, I had to do so much more than the administration textbooks indicate. I played an important part in both of those communities—inside and outside the school. That is the best preparation for what schools have to deal with today." Marsha has not, however, attended any classes or workshops for at least 5 years, nor is she active in any professional associations. Because several of her colleagues and some of her teachers question whether she has kept up with the rapidly changing national scene of education today, her case represents the need a principal has for continued professional development.

Beyond the CAP schools, another principal of a school that is involved in a variety of change efforts reports that every year he attends summer programs offered by the principals' center at a respected university to enhance his professional growth. One year he was a principal-in-residence at this center.

Summary

Tomorrow's principals will likely continue to come from two traditional sources: teachers and other administrators already working in schools. If they are to be principals-in-charge of dynamic schools, they will require preparation programs that recognize their individual needs, ensure their mastery of specific skills and understandings, and develop their ability to discover and apply knowledge. In addition to building skills and knowledge, the principal-in-charge must develop orientations that shape a dynamic school. They must be socialized to see themselves as facilitators of internal processes, as managers of the environment, and as leaders of an evaluation-minded school; they must understand the social, historical, and world context of education today.

Preparation programs will use alternative modes to prepare these leaders for their new roles and to enable them to maintain their momentum of learning and growing professionally. Depending on their background, different candidates will need different preparation. For example, empowered teachers already working in dynamic schools will probably already have the internal and evaluation orientations but will need to look outward to develop entrepreneurial orientations. On the other hand, principals of traditional schools probably will already be familiar with fiscal processes and traditional evaluation procedures, but will need to develop the orientations that will enable them to lead dynamic schools.

Most important, however, is the conceptualization of leadership training as a continuous process. Preparing leaders is not a linear path with a single starting point and ending point. Rather, the process is more of a revolving door that includes both formal and informal activities and that has multiple entry and exit points. The principal is, in fact, socialized over time, acquiring knowledge, skills, beliefs, and dispositions. Principals of dynamic schools are socialized to accept responsibility for their ongoing professional renewal and development. Developing leaders of dynamic schools, then, is an aspect of the lifelong learning of these professionals, and opportunities must exist to accommodate and support this notion.

8

The Leader

Taking Charge of Change

How do principals of dynamic schools feel about their work? How do they see their roles as leaders of a new kind of school? This chapter looks at the composite principal-in-charge—the principal in all the roles. We present Lee and other principals-in-charge as leaders, ones who process and learn from their experiences, ones who make conscious choices about improving their schools.

"Seeing you guys really made a difference for me today," said Ginny, another principal of a dynamic school. "Sometimes I feel so alone, so overwhelmed."

"Same for me," agreed Andrew. "When we talk, I believe again—that our schools really are making strides. But there are times when I am trying to work with parents, teachers, the regulations, and mandates—and there's the central office because, supportive as he is, my super isn't always a help—they all want results—*now*—I just get to feeling I cannot keep it up."

Lee, Ginny, and Andrew were sitting together at a meeting of the regional consortium for school improvement. The alliance had formed so that leaders of schools engaged in school improvement efforts might gather, share experiences, and learn new approaches. These three principals met at early meetings of the consortium and formed a friendship based on their mutual recognition that they each shared a similar view of their roles as principals of changing schools.

"You know, you just mentioned results. Sometimes I think *results* are our real enemy," Lee said, thinking aloud. "The kind of changes we are trying to bring about will take a long time. I think we will be lucky if we have the kind of schools we envision in 20 years—but everybody seems to want things to happen yesterday. I often feel that half of my energy goes into showing people that things are better—when not much has actually changed yet!"

"I see it another way. People want results, but they don't really want change. They want to believe everything is as it was in the good ol' days, and here we are, throwing it in their faces how different the world is and suggesting that they look at schools in a very different light," said Ginny. "We are admitting that families aren't all like Dick and Jane's, that not everybody speaks English, that some kids have handicaps, that drugs and alcohol and gangs and teenage pregnancy are real. We are telling them that teachers can take more responsibility, that parents should play a greater role in the decision making, that the community must provide more resources—that all must share in the accountability."

"Maybe the real problem is that we can't be perfect—and I am not being funny," protested Andrew. "To move our schools forward as we think they ought to, we have a diverse set of responsibilities. And I will tell you that I don't do all of them well—I can't, not even most of the time!"

"I'll say! Last week, to give just one example, I really blew it with the teachers' union," Ginny admitted. "They had clashed with the parent volunteers, and I took the volunteers' side—I didn't see that the teachers weren't ready to look at parents in new roles. The union nearly filed a grievance. We did work it out, but I sure lost a lot of trust. No, I don't always handle situations well."

"Coordinating all the teams gets me crazy at times, because they each may be at different stages," Lee said. "My evaluation-coordination team has really bought the concept of an evaluation-minded, self-correcting school, but not all of the other teams—or individuals, for that matter—are ready to see that evaluation can be more helpful than threatening. One of the teacher assistance teams refused to let the other team see any of its records—they were afraid that they would be scored on how many problems they had solved. I guess we have a long way to go."

"So that brings me back to where I started," Ginny said, smiling. "I do believe it's worth the hard work. All I need is to hear that I am not alone—that you are going through the same things. And to have you remind me that we aren't going to change schools overnight!"

Lee agreed, "We do need each other. And that's why this group continues to meet. We are principals who are choosing to change. Our changes won't make a difference until a noticeable group of schools operates differently. While we are not yet a critical mass, we are working on it!"

"And who knows?" Andrew said with a laugh. "Maybe in less than 20 years we will be toasting the predominance of the schools we are working for—schools that tap the unique resources of our communities to establish environments in which everyone can grow and learn!"

*　　*　　*

Principals like Lee are a new type of principal. These principals-in-charge draw on many of the traditional skills of a principal, but they see their roles differently: They are facilitators, balancers, flag bearers and bridgers, and inquirers who are growing professionally. They take on these roles because they see that the world is different, and they choose to capitalize on these differences. Their schools also are different; dynamic schools engage in ongoing processes of change for improvement. The task of creating improved learning environments for students in these schools is not completed. Rather, they are schools in transition. Leadership in these schools is complex, challenging, and not always successful, but these principals are taking clear stands and responsibility for improving the learning environments of their schools.

We see that Lee is not alone; other principals of dynamic schools are also working to support changes that will make schools better places for teachers to teach and students to learn. Not every principal-in-charge succeeds in every endeavor, nor does each one possess every skill necessary to lead these changing schools. Although they share similar visions, they do not necessarily use the same approach to achieve that vision. Their actions vary according to their individual strengths and the needs of their particular schools and communities. All, however, acknowledge the forces at work changing today's schools. And all are reflective practitioners (Schon, 1983); that is, they all question and process and learn from their experiences. Most important, they are reflective leaders: They examine their situations, make choices, and work with others to enable goals to be reached.

These principals, whom we have called principals-in-charge, do exist in various forms. We have seen them in what we have labeled as dynamic schools. On-site while collecting data for the evaluations of CAP and for the Coalition case study, we have seen principals display the behaviors we attribute to these leaders. During interviews for the study of the LRE initiative, we have heard principals describe other behaviors and attitudes that fit our image of principals-in-charge. Through analyses of the *High School and Beyond* (USDE, 1984) data set, we have constructed a corroborating picture of these principals and their schools. Finally, the literature on improving schools from the past decade offers examples that support our conceptualization of the dynamic school and its leader. While no one individual demonstrates all the characteristics and fulfills all the roles of a Lee, individuals who demonstrate enough to be identified as principals-in-charge are functioning in schools that are engaged in a number of positive change efforts.

The schools we chose from the CAP, Coalition, and LRE studies are all succeeding with the specific program or programs they have chosen to implement to improve their learning environments. Still, these dynamic schools are ones whose changes are in process. They are in continuing transition, and their goals are for the long term, not one-shot, quick fixes. For example, the successful CAP schools were concerned with much more than reducing the numbers of students identified as learning disabled; they were using the program to change attitudes about learning problems and practices to address these problems. Because they are evaluation-minded schools, they have built in feedback mechanisms so that they may be self-correcting; that is, they review their programs and make changes where and as needed. They know that results may not be immediate, but they monitor what is happening, so that they may make judgments about what is happening.

Because we have looked at schools that are engaged in these long-term changes, we have not looked at student achievement or specific school outcomes. The changes are still in progress and not all outcomes are visible. Put simply, dynamic schools have not reached all their goals yet. Therefore, the focus of this volume has been on the principals of these schools, the persons whose leadership enables these processes.

Some school critics have espoused a decreased need for leadership in the form of a principal (e.g., Gursky, 1990). They note empowered teachers, school-site councils, and the existing hierarchy, and they ask why a principal is needed. Our view is that in schools with empowered teachers and enfranchised parents principals-in-charge are even more important than in the traditional school organization.

In this chapter, we will review the forces that have an impact on schools and reexamine the leadership roles used by principals-in-charge to lead dynamic schools, the schools responding to these forces. We will also consider the difficulties and realities of being a principal of a dynamic school.

Forces Changing Schools

A school that is truly changing needs a principal who can articulate a vision, provide direction, facilitate those who are working for the change, coordinate the different groups, and balance the various forces impacting schools today. Principals-in-charge are such leaders. While much of what they do is similar to the work of a traditional principal, principals-in-charge approach their work differently. First, they recognize the forces that impact schools and education today, and second, they use these forces as resources rather than hindrances or burdens.

We believe that five major forces are changing the ways in which principals must lead and manage their schools. Teachers' responsibilities are extending beyond their classrooms and their students. Collaborative problem-solving teams, site-based management, career ladders, and differentiated staffing structures offer new possibilities for teachers to be highly involved in school improvement processes.

Student bodies are increasingly diverse. This diversity is no longer limited to cultural, racial, or ethnic differences. Schools and their leaders are challenged with meeting the wide range of needs of all students. The changing social and economic characteristics of families add other dimensions to the complexities of the student bodies that schools must serve.

Parents are more vocal and more involved in schools. Many reform efforts specify a parental involvement component. Even in schools where parental involvement is not driven by such reforms, parents as individuals or organized groups are increasingly acting as either advocates or adversaries. No longer are principals solely leaders of other professionals; they are now leaders of a wider school community.

The social, technological, and communal contexts of schools are more complex. Schools can no longer close their doors on their surroundings. They are expected to help meet the total needs of both the children and their communities. These social needs include new demands and pressures from employers that require a different type of graduate than in the past. Principals are crucial links between schools and their external contexts.

Finally, the relationship between the state and the local district concerning educational reform is changing. While in the past states have often left matters to local districts, today they are mandating programs and standards in response to national education reports of the 1980s. Principals must respond to these state mandates while simultaneously cultivating school-based, local initiatives.

Throughout this volume we illustrate that principals-in-charge choose to manage these forces that are impacting their schools. "Change is not something that happens only to schools. But it is a force educators must learn to manage effectively if they are to recreate schools to meet the needs of the 21st century" (Sparks, 1992, p. 22). Principals-in-charge engage empowered teachers as instructional decision makers. They turn enfranchised parents and involved community agencies into support capital. They visualize diversity as enrichment. They use technology to solve problems, and they use mandates to legitimize ongoing changes. In sum, they are conscious of the forces of society on their schools, and they make conscious decisions to act on these forces. They make time to reflect and act.

Changing Leadership Roles

Principals of dynamic schools see their work as complex, consisting of several interdependent roles interacting with the different internal and external constituencies we have described in the previous chapters. They are not simply leaders; rather, they are leaders because they are facilitators, balancers, flag bearers and bridgers, and inquirers. Finally, they listen, they reflect, and they take stands on issues. They recognize that although all these forces and constituencies are resources, the proverbial buck stops with them. They, as principals of dynamic schools, are ultimately responsible. Thus teams, councils, and advisory groups may have input, but the responsibility for any final decision lies with the principal. And with them lies the responsibility to see that decisions are carried out. They recognize that, as principals, they are in charge, but only after they have reflected on the variety of input available to them through their different roles.

The Facilitator

As facilitators, principals-in-charge create the conditions whereby those working in their schools may accomplish tasks with a strong sense of personal efficacy. These facilitators motivate, coordinate, and legitimize the work of their teachers by taking stands based on consideration and understanding of participants' positions on issues and then by manipulating time, space, resources, and personnel to join in moving toward the attainment of that position. Decisions may be made collaboratively, but someone must be in charge of seeing that those decisions are implemented. In short, the facilitator enables others to act and legitimizes their actions.

We have used Lee as the prototype facilitator, and we offer several illustrations of real principals acting as facilitators. Perhaps the most complete example of a principal-in-charge succeeding as a facilitator is Eileen, whose classroom alternative support team at the Tipton Elementary School saw that reading continually appeared as the source of student learning problems at the primary level. Based on the team's input, she took the position that the situation could be remedied through the replacement of the K-3 textbooks with readable, interesting trade books. Armed with supportive data, she took this decision to the school board and won its approval—and the necessary resources. Her manipulation produced the resources, and the legitimation, for the teachers to make major changes in the school's reading program. In other words, Eileen facilitated a group of empowered teachers.

Eileen's example is an ideal case; she and the teachers agreed on the approach, and the desired change was reasonable and possible. Eileen herself noted that she could not always agree with team decisions, often because she had access to contradictory input either from within the system or from external sources. Still, as a good facilitator, she was present to share her concerns and her perceptions of the barriers.

In some cases, the facilitator needs to accept the team's decision and support its attainment, as did Lee when the Vibrant Springs planning team chose to deal with alternative scheduling instead of outcome assessment. Lee understood the team's reasoning and worked on the plan to ensure that it was workable. Whatever the situation, the principal facilitator is in charge, listening, making choices, and carrying out plans.

One role, then, that the leader of a dynamic school takes on is that of the facilitator, the enabler of internal leadership. This role is, however, tightly linked to another role for the principal-in-charge, the balancer, the translator within the system hierarchy.

The Balancer

To facilitate internal leadership and decision making, the principal of a dynamic school balances autonomy for the school with influence and control from the system hierarchy. Balancers recognize that they and their schools are part of a system hierarchy so their decisions will be influenced by educational partners outside the school walls but within the system. As balancers, the principals of dynamic schools make choices about priorities and build relationships that will foster those decisions. In this position, knowledge becomes a resource; much of their time is spent communicating—listening, translating, informing, and filtering. This communication is important to establishing the principal-in-charge's vision or position.

Perhaps the strongest relationship in this communication process is the one between the principal-in-charge and the superintendent. The principal aims to build mutually defined goals with the superintendent so that one can support the other. Early in the process, Lee, as our prototype balancer, brings to the superintendent the school's decision to move to alternative scheduling; Marty offers support at the board meeting and is willing to pave the way for exemptions of state certification requirements. But to get this support, Lee has to be sure that Vibrant Springs's plans and demands do not run counter to the philosophy or vision of the central office.

Both Ken and Eileen illustrate this skill of balancing autonomy and influence. Ken wants to reorganize programs to eliminate honors sections; because he is in close contact with his superintendent, he knows that the planning teams proposal will need to be modified to get the superintendent's support before the board. Eileen knows the state-supported literacy initiative encourages the use of trade books over basal readers for the primary level. She and Randy, her superintendent, have been active in the curriculum group; therefore, she knows she can expect support when she takes the team's plan to the local board. Ken and Eileen, like Lee, know what they want and build relationships within their system hierarchies to achieve their goals. The principal of a dynamic school, then, takes on the role of balancer as well as facilitator.

The Flag Bearer and Bridger

Another role for this leader, the flag bearer and bridger, links the school to the external environment. Because a dynamic school has a plan and stands for something, the principal is in charge of carrying the message to the community in which the school lives. These principals acknowledge the impact of their environments on their ability to accomplish their goals, so they work to communicate and build relationships with community constituencies that will serve to support their school's internal activities. In this way, the principal of a dynamic school is a flag bearer. But the community also has a message to bring to the school. Again, the principal-in-charge assumes the role of building the bridges so that these messages are transmitted and managed.

Building this delicate relationship with the school's environment is the crucial task of the bridger. At times, it is necessary to keep the school's independence from environmental input and influence. Independence and autonomy are often achieved by buffering. At other times, widespread cooperation is developed between the school and its environment through such partnerships as contracting, cooptation, and coalition building. The principal is in charge of environmental information, serving as filter, facilitator, and disseminator. Typically, Lee illustrates these skills through interaction with various individuals and groups in the community; Lee collects information and then makes decisions about what and where to pass on. We have seen Mike, interviewed for the LRE study, choose those voices of parents that advocated the school's stand on inclusion from among the many advocacy groups present in the community. Mike was in charge of the information and knew how to use it, because he knew what the school wanted.

In a dynamic school, boundaries between the external and internal worlds are breaking down; parents and representatives from community businesses and agencies participate in decision-making processes and offer a variety of other inputs. Especially under these conditions, the school needs a strong principal to give direction and to move the decisions into action. A parent in Cotter School, a CAP school that also used shared decision making on a principal's advisory team, commented about the principal: "I think we'd be wasting our time if Hugh wasn't in charge. I mean, otherwise, we'd just sit around and talk—and spend all our time figuring out how we're gonna be making decisions."

Principals of dynamic schools must be in charge of building the bridges between their schools and the surrounding world, and they must bear their schools' flags across those bridges as well as welcome across those who can develop and support the mission of the school. Thus the role of flag bearer and bridger is added to the list of roles for the principal of a dynamic school. However, to ensure accomplishing all these roles, the final role for principals-in-charge asks them to look back into the school to evaluate the effects of their leadership.

The Inquirer

Principals-in-charge question where their schools have gone, where they are going, and their progress in getting there. As inquirer, the principal takes charge of an evaluation-minded school, modeling behaviors that encourage the asking of questions and the use of systematically collected data. In this role, the principal leads the processes of collaborative problem solving and shared decision making.

Although the evaluation processes are coordinated by a team designated for this effort, the principal can make or break the effort. Again, Lee serves as the prototype: open-minded and willing to surface and address weaknesses and support strengths to find answers. This type of principal establishes the atmosphere in which an inquiry ethic is possible. In all of the dynamic schools we looked at, the principal's leadership in this area was crucial—all demonstrated in words and actions that they examined themselves and their schools' activities with a critical eye.

The role of inquirer may be the most difficult to sustain over time; long-term self-critique and critique of those programs and people that are self-initiated or self-facilitated can be ego deflating. The rewards can, however, be important because they can encourage progress along the path to school improvement. The principal-in-charge sees that evaluation data are used formatively to alter programs and procedures in place and that summative data are collected and used appropriately. The principal-in-charge sees that hard decisions are enacted based on what the data reveal.

Principals of dynamic schools ensure that they are evaluated as facilitators, as balancers, as flag bearers and bridgers, and finally as inquirers. And they ensure that the work that they enable is assessed: Are decisions being reached? Are the plans being enacted? Are desired goals being reached? In sum, as inquirer, the principal-in-charge must ask, "Where is my leadership taking this school? Is this where we want to go?"

The Learner

The role of inquirer involves being a learner. The education of a principal-in-charge is neither a continual nor a one-time process. We characterized the process as a revolving door; principals enter and exit, learning experiences at various times, developing orientations that enable them to perform the roles we describe. These orientations encourage continual learning and reflection in addition to action. As a leader who is in charge and who also reflects and learns, the principal of a dynamic school inspires other members of the school to be reflective practitioners. Principals-in-charge rely on both formal and informal mechanisms for learning and reflection. The principal serves as a role model, establishing an atmosphere in which all members of the school's organization work to improve the processes and outcomes. In this way, the principal encourages a self-correcting school.

The Leader

Being a principal of a dynamic school is not easy. The reality of a changing environment presents many challenges to these leaders. The tasks are complex and often appear overwhelming. No blueprint exists for the ideal principal-in-charge—although

Lee serves as a prototype, Lee is a composite. We have seen no one individual who has all the attributes of a Lee. Each principal-in-charge is unique; each makes decisions and choices based on an individual reading of the school's different contexts. Because they have no maps to follow, they must often take risks. Sometimes they win; sometimes they lose. But they continue to make choices that they believe will lead to an improved school.

Dynamic schools are not geared toward revolutionizing the structure of America's schools. Rather in dynamic schools principals-in-charge acknowledge that the focus of change must be the processes of educational leadership, not merely the bureaucratic structure of schools. The implementation of new processes of educational leadership will simultaneously change the controlling nature of schools. It is the processes of educational leadership, such as the nature of decision making, that are altered in dynamic schools.

Principals-in-charge of a dynamic school must attend to more constituencies than do principals of traditional schools. Although empowered teachers assume some of the functions previously relegated to a principal, the principal still must coordinate these functions as well as attend to other groups impacting the school. In seeking for and enacting creative solutions, the principal-in-charge needs to have a stronger, more intense relationship with the superintendent and central office; thus he or she spends more time informing, negotiating with, and discussing with those in the system hierarchy than would a traditional principal who tends to follow directives. With more permeable boundaries between the dynamic school and the environment, the principal deals with more and different groups of parents, business representatives, and community agencies. The principal is still usually the first contact point with the external environment but will most likely spend more energy with these constituencies than traditional principals who focus most of their efforts internally.

Reform efforts in education, such as school-based management and schools of public choice have increased both the legitimacy and quantity of the involvement of external constituencies in school affairs. However, these reforms have not eliminated the hierarchical governing structure of most school systems. Consequently, principals-in-charge, as they engage more frequently with external groups, must simultaneously continue to consider their superiors at the central office and other influential bodies, such as school boards, state and federal governments, and the courts.

In their organizational reality, principals often serve as mediators between the schools numerous constituencies. Principals

> must simultaneously manage at least four sets of relationships: upward, with their superiors, downward with subordinates, laterally with other principals and externally, with parents and other community and business groups. This configuration of relationships is very complex in that managing one set of relationships successfully may interfere with or hinder another set of relationships. Furthermore, each of these role partners may have different, often conflicting, expectations of the principal. (Goldring, 1993. p. 95)

Principals-in-charge must be acutely aware of their political and organizational environments. Ultimately, these environments have enormous impact on the extent to which principals can be in charge.

Dynamic schools require that the internal roles, responsibilities, and relationships among all school professionals be altered. Decision making, planning, and implementation of programs must be school based. Site-based management is one possible mechanism to change such role relationships. These types of changes are difficult and have long-term consequences. As Cambon, Weiss, and Wyeth (1992) suggested in a recent study of teachers' thoughts about school-based decision making, "teachers need thoughtful guidance from their leaders in the ways of shared decision making, in gaining skill and tolerance for consensus building, conflict resolution and perspective taking" (p. 58). Thus principals-in-charge must attend to the teachers, working with the staff to articulate a shared vision, guiding them to help their schools change.

The principal-in-charge remains the primary source of accountability, a major reality in the dynamic school, possibly more so than in regular schools. Dynamic schools present themselves as places of change. The public, essentially conservative about the institution of schools, remains skeptical and expects results. That many of the changes will require years to produce desired outcomes and that those results may not be dramatic or even available at early stages are of no matter to a critical public. The principal of a dynamic school must find honest but creative ways to satisfy those demands.

Finally, the principal of a dynamic school must face these challenges with few colleagues. A critical mass of dynamic schools with reflective leaders does not yet exist. Although networks such as the Coalition of Essential Schools and Phil Schlecty's Quality Schools have formed and offer support and resources, a changing school is still an anomaly. Until the public expects to see schools that have broken traditional molds, the job of the leader of a dynamic school will be lonely and difficult.

Summary

Principals of dynamic schools know themselves—their strengths and limitations, their passions and their indifferences. They embrace the forces in their environments and interpret the voices within their communities. Thus they consciously make choices and act on them. Having looked deeply into their communities, they articulate the wishes of the constituencies. As leaders, they take stands within their communities and inspire others to act with them. They are principals-in-charge.

Dynamic schools and their leaders serve as catalysts for many changes. These developments require complex analysis and questioning. Future discussions should consider the implications of this type of leadership for the system hierarchy and others responsible for school governance. How do principals-in-charge influence the bureaucratic structure of school systems? Does this require simultaneous changes in the roles of school boards? Furthermore, analysis should study the implications of this type of leadership for the principals themselves. How can the momentum be sustained? What are the constraints? Are there any unintended consequences associated with the dynamic school? Our framework sets the agenda for such discussions.

The turbulence that social change has affected in schools requires new leaders. Principals-in-charge represent the best hope for school leadership of the future. Challenging and multidimensional, principals-in-charge set goals and standards and capture what leadership can be.

APPENDIX

Data Sources and Methods

This appendix describes the methods used in the CAP study, the LRE study, the case study of the principal in a changing school for the Coalition of Essential Schools, and the *High School and Beyond* (USDE, 1984) data set. What were the purposes? How were sites selected? How were data collected and analyzed? How were the findings reported?

The Classroom Alternative Process Evaluation Study

CAP, a federally funded statewide initiative, was designed to address strategies for regular education teachers to remediate students' problems before or instead of referral to special education. The project was implemented through the Rhode Island Department of Education (RIDE) in two pilot communities during the 1985-1986 school year and spread to schools of all levels throughout the state during following years. CAP involved the establishment of school-based problem-solving teams made up of teachers, counselors, and administrators at each school. The actual composition of each classroom alternative support team (CAST) as well as specific operating procedures were determined by the schools themselves. The building principal was a member of the team in most schools. Training and follow-up technical assistance was provided by RIDE's Special Education Program Services Unit.

In the first stages of the project implementation, the Center for Evaluation and Research of Rhode Island College was contracted to provide evaluation services for the project. Rallis was the primary evaluator and director of the evaluation. Project personnel worked closely with the evaluator from the start. They identified two major purposes for the evaluation: to provide formative feedback to improve the program's operation in the schools and to document the program's impact on the schools, teachers, and children involved. Data collection began in the two pilot districts in fall 1985 and grew to cover the 61 schools that had been trained by spring 1989. Evaluation activities included the following:

- Longitudinal (1985-1989) quantitative documentation of the identification of students with handicaps
- Analysis of the Case Status Record Keeper, which tracked all cases referred to teams in all buildings
- Interviews with CAST chairpersons and principals in pilot and other selected schools
- Administration over 3 years of questionnaires to all teachers who had referred a student to the CAST
- Administration over 2 years of questionnaires to all CAST members
- Administration and analysis of a preschool and postschool climate survey to teachers and administrators in all pilot schools
- End-of-training evaluations of the RIDE-sponsored training from all teachers and principals who had participated

Instruments were designed to assess implementation and perceptions of utility of the process. Specifically, the evaluation focused on the contextual variables under which teams operated and on the changing attitudes within the schools. Using constructive analytic procedures, we combined inductive category coding with comparison across categories (Glaser & Strauss, 1967). Schools were categorized according to level of team functioning, and the contextual variables were identified within and compared across categories. Data collected from different sources were triangulated. Results indicated that the teams functioned in dynamic schools and offered images of principals who empowered teachers, dealt with problems collaboratively, created resources where none existed, and coped with diverse student populations with multiple needs.

Findings were reported in a series of newsletters to CAST members and in a summative evaluation report to RIDE for the State Board of Regents for Elementary and Secondary Education. For further details on instrumentation, analyses, and interpretation see Center for Evaluation and Research (1989).

The Least Restrictive Environment Initiative Study

The LRE initiative in Rhode Island is a federally supported effort to integrate students with disabilities into regular education classrooms. As one activity in the state's LRE initiative, RIDE's Special Education Program Services Unit launched a major effort to train building principals in new ways of thinking about serving the students in their buildings. The training acknowledged that the school principal, as instructional leader, is responsible for the education of all students, both regular and special education, in the building. The aim of this training was to enable principals to set new goals for leadership that would include all students.

RIDE contracted an evaluator (Rallis) to interview a selection of principals who had participated in the training and in whose buildings at least some LRE activities were operating. A total of 10 principals (one has since become a coordinator of elementary education in her district), representing seven communities, were interviewed individually. The seven communities included three of the major cities in the state, two towns, one rural district, and one suburb. Four of the five LRE pilot districts were included. Interview questions sought to determine the following:

- Principals' orientations toward special needs students and any changes in these orientations since LRE was introduced in the state
- Changes that may have occurred in building practices related to special needs placement
- Factors that may have contributed to these changes

Interviews were transcribed and analyzed with the ethnographic approach (Hammersley & Atkinson, 1983; Spradley, 1979) using the constant comparative method (Glaser & Strauss, 1967). The intensive interviews conducted with the principals in these schools yielded pictures of men and women who recognized the forces in a changing social context and were taking risks to harness those forces to improve their schools (Rallis, 1991). Some principals were more successful than others, but each was trying to work with teachers and parents to facilitate change.

The analysis of the findings was reported to the RIDE's Special Education Unit spring 1991, in both a presentation and a summary report (Rallis, 1991).

The Case Study for the Coalition of Essential Schools

The Coalition of Essential Schools is a network of schools, primarily secondary schools, that collaborate and support each other as they implement the Nine Common Principles presented in *Horace's Compromise* (Sizer, 1984). The central offices of the coalition are located at Brown University, Providence, Rhode Island. Having taken an intensive look at teachers' ways of understanding and enacting school change (see, e.g., Wasley, 1991, which is based on a monograph printed by the coalition), the coalition chose to look also at principals in changing schools. The coalition asked Rallis to study Ken Wilkerson, principal of Midway High School, because it saw him as a principal who is making changes happen in his school. The coalition wanted a portrait of such a leader for use in training workshops to guide discussions on leadership for positive change. To paint such a portrait, Rallis (1992) followed Ken, watching him act and interact; I talked with him at length to question and probe his thoughts. I watched his school, observing hallways, classrooms, and various student gatherings. I spoke with his faculty, informally in the lunchroom and restrooms, and formally in meetings or interviews. I listened to and heard a variety of conversations. (p. 1)

Data collection included two intensive ethnographic interviews (of at least 2 hours duration) that were transcribed and analyzed. All interviews and observations were conducted and analyzed using a narrative inquiry process (Connelly & Clandinin, 1990), focusing on both the individual and the context using the constant comparative method. To write the final portrait, Rallis drew on the conceptualization and example of portraiture offered by Lightfoot (1983). The portrait of Ken (Rallis, 1992) is available from the Coalition of Essential Schools at Brown University.

The *High School and Beyond* Data Set

The original *High School and Beyond* (USDE, 1984) study included 60,000 students in about 1,000 secondary schools and aimed to learn about student achievement, attitudes, activities, and family background. The survey of principals, developed by the National Center for Education Statistics at the U.S. Department of Education, was administered to a national sample of approximately 50% of the original schools that had participated in the *High School and Beyond* study, namely 532 secondary schools. A total of 76% (402) of the principals returned the questionnaire. The questionnaire asked principals a wide array of questions regarding their relationships with teachers and external role partners, their school structure, sense of autonomy, educational practices, and their latitude of influence. The analyses presented in this book are based on the responses from public school principals only.

The typical principal in the *High School and Beyond* study is male, with 15 years of teaching experience. He has been a principal for about 10 years and has been working in his present school for 6 years. He has been principal in about three other schools as well.

Dynamic Schools

Coalition School

Midway High School
    a suburban district
    Ken is principal; Bob is superintendent

CAP Study Schools

Tipton Elementary
    an industrial, urban district
    Eileen is principal; Randy is superintendent

Hope Street Elementary
    a small city district (same district as Ashland)
    Jim is principal; Matt is superintendent

Ashland Elementary
    small city district (same district as Hope Street)
    Larry is principal; Matt is superintendent

Chilton Junior High School
    a rural, regional district
    Paul is principal

Littleton K-8
    a rural school
    Marsha is principal

Central Middle School
    an urban district
    Roger is principal

LRE Study Schools

Stewart Elementary (also a CAP school)
    an urban district
    Mike is principal

Willowtree (also a CAP school)
    a rural district
    Anita is principal; Pete is superintendent

Cotter Elementary School
   a suburban district
   Hugh is principal
Alton Valley K-6 School
   a residential section of city district
   Sarah is one of the faculty; Art is principal

References

Ainscow, M. (1991). *Effective schools for all.* London: David Fulton.

Aldrich, H., & Herker, D. (1977). Boundary spanning roles and organizational structure. *Academy of Management Review, 2,* 217-230.

Andrews, R., & Soder, R. (1987). Principal instructional leadership and school achievement. *Instructional Leadership, 44,* 9-11.

Bacharach, S. B. (1981). Organization and political dimensions for research on school district governance and administration. In S. B. Bacharach (Ed.), *Organizational behavior in schools and school districts* (pp. 3-43). New York: Praeger.

Bacharach, S. B., & Shedd, J. B. (1989). Power and empowerment: The constraining myths and emerging structures of teacher unionism in an age of reform. In J. Hannaway & R. Crowson (Eds.), *The politics of reforming school administration* (pp. 139-160). New York: Falmer.

Barth, R. S. (1986). Principal centered professional development. *Theory-into-Practice, 25*(3), 156-160.

Barth, R. S. (1990). *Improving schools from within.* San Francisco: Jossey-Bass.

Bauch, P. (1989). *Family choice, parent involvement in inner-city Catholic high schools: An exploration of parent psycho-social and school organizational factors.* Unpublished manuscript, Catholic University, Washington, DC.

Beck, L., & Murphy, J. (1993). *Understanding the principalship: A metaphorical analysis from 1920-1990.* New York: Teachers College Press.

Becker, H. J., & Epstein, J. L. (1982). Parent involvement: A study of teacher practices. *Elementary School Journal, 83,* 85-102.

Berman, P., & McLaughlin, M. W. (1975). *Federal programs supporting educational change: The findings in review* (Vol. 4). Santa Monica, CA: Rand.

Berman, P., & McLaughlin, M. W. (1978). *Federal programs supporting educational change: Implementing and sustaining innovation* (Vol. 8). Santa Monica, CA: Rand.

Blase, J. J. (1989). Teachers' political orientations vis-à-vis the principal: The micropolitics of the schools. In J. Hannaway & R. Crowson (Eds.), *The politics of reforming school administration* (pp. 113-126). New York: Falmer.

Bolman, L. G., & Deal, T. E. (1984). *Modern approaches to understanding organizations.* San Francisco: Jossey-Bass.

Bolman, L. G., & Deal, T. E. (1991). *Reframing organizations.* San Francisco: Jossey Bass.

Bossert, S., Dwyer, D., Rowan, B., & Lee, G. (1982). The instructional management role of the principal. *Educational Administration Quarterly, 18,* 36-64.

Boyan, N. (1988). Describing and explaining administrator behavior. In N. Boyan (Ed.), *Handbook of research on educational administration* (pp. 77-98). New York: Longman.

Bredeson, P. (1989, March 27-31). *Redefining leadership and the roles of school principals: Responses to changes in the professional worklife of teachers.* Paper presented at the Annual Meeting of the American Educational Research Association, San Francisco.

Bridges, E. M. (1977). The nature of leadership. In L. Cunningham, W. Hack, & R. Nystrand (Eds.), *Educational administration: The developing decades* (pp. 202-230). Berkeley, CA: McCutchan.

Bridges, E. M. (1992). *Problem-based learning for administrators* (with the assistance of P. Hallinger). Eugene, OR: ERIC Clearinghouse on Educational Management.

Bryk, A. S., & Driscoll, M. E. (1988). *The high school as community: Contextual influences, and consequences for students and teachers.* Madison, WI: National Center on Effective Secondary Schools.

Burns, T., & Stalker, G. M. (1961). *The management of innovation.* London: Tavistock.

Caldwell, B. J. (1990). School leadership in a new era of management in public education. In P. W. Thurston & L. S. Lotto (Eds.), *Advances in educational administration* (Vol. 1B, pp. 41-71). Greenwich, CT: JAI.

California State Department of Education, Bilingual Education Office. (1986). *Beyond language: Social and cultural factors in schooling language minority students.* Los Angeles: Evaluation, Dissemination, and Assessment Center.

Cambon, J., Weiss, C. M., & Wyeth, A. (1992, October). *We're not programmed for this: An exploration of the variance between the ways teachers think and the concepts of shared decision making in high schools* (National Center for Educational Leadership Occasional Paper No. 17). Boston: Harvard University.

Carini, P. (1986). *The Prospect Center documentary processes: In progress.* Bennington, VT: Prospect Archive and Center for Education and Research.

Carnegie Task Force on Teaching as a Profession. (1986). *A nation prepared: Teachers for the 21st century.* New York: Carnegie Forum on Education and the Economy.

Center for Evaluation and Research. (1989, August). *The learning disabilities identification project: Summative evaluation results, The Rhode Island Department of Education, Special Education Program Services Unit (Technical report).* Providence: Center for Evaluation and Research, Rhode Island College.

Chapman, J. D. (1990). School-based decision-making and management: Implication for school personnel. In J. D. Chapman (Ed.), *School-based decision-making and management* (pp. 221-144). London: Falmer.

Chen, M., & Goldring, E. (1990). *Principals' resources and their annual implementation of first order reform efforts.* Paper presented at the annual meeting of the University Council of Educational Administration, Pittsburgh.

Chen, M., & Goldring, E. (1992). *Aspiring teacher-leaders and school change: Black sheep or white knights.* Paper presented at the International Congress on School Effectiveness and School Improvement, Victoria, CA.

Cibulka, J. G. (1988). *Autonomy, environments and leadership: Comparisons among Catholic high schools.* Paper presented at the annual meeting of the American Educational Research Association, New Orleans.

Cibulka, J. G. (1989). State performance incentives for restructuring: Can they work? *Education and Urban Society, 21*(4), 417-435.

Clark, D. L., Lotto, L. S., & Astito, T. A. (1984). Effective schools and school improvement: A comparative analysis of two lines of inquiry. *Educational Administration Quarterly, 20*, 41-68.

Clark, D. L., Lotto, L., & McCarthy, M. M. (1980). Factors associated with success in urban elementary schools. *Phi Delta Kappan, 61*, 467-470.

Coleman, J. S. (1987). Families and schools. *Educational Researcher, 16*, 32-38.

Coleman, J. S., & Hoffer, T. (1986). *Public and private high schools.* New York: Basic.

Coleman, P., & LaRocque, L. (1990). *Struggling to be good enough.* London: Falmer.

Conger, J., & Kanungo, R. (1988). The empowerment process: Integrating theory and practice. *Academy of Management Review, 13*, 471-482.

Conley, S. C. (1988). Reforming paper pushers and avoiding free agents. *Educational Administration Quarterly, 24*, 393-404.

Conley, S. C. (1990). A metaphor for teaching: Beyond the bureaucratic professional dichotomy. In S. B. Bacharach (Ed.), *Educational reform* (pp. 313-324). Boston: Allen & Bacon.

Connelly, F. M., & Clandinin, D. J. (1990, June-July). Stories of experience and narrative inquiry. *Educational Researcher, 19*(5), 2-14.

Cooley, V. E. (1993, January). Tips for implementing a student assistance program. *NASSP Bulletin, 6*(549), 10-17.

Corwin, R. G. (1965). *A sociology of education.* New York: Appleton Century Crofts.

Cromer, J. (1984). *High tech schools: The principals' perspective* (Report of the National Association of Secondary School Principals). Reston, VA: NASSP.

Crow, G. (1991). *The principal in schools of choice: Middle manager, entrepreneur, and symbol manager.* Paper presented at the annual meeting of the American Educational Research Association, Chicago.

Crow, G., Mecklowitz, B., & Weekes, Y. (1992). From teaching to administration: A preparation institute. *Journal of School Leadership, 2,* 188-200.

Crowson, R. L. (1988). Editor's introduction. The local school district superintendency under reform. *Peabody Journal of Education, 65,* 1-8.

Crowson, R. L., & Boyd, W. L. (1992). *Coordinated services for children: Designing arks for storms and seas unknown.* Philadelphia: National Center for Education in the Inner Cities, Temple University.

Crowson, R. L., & Morris, V. C. (1992). The superintendency and school effectiveness: An organizational hierarchy perspective. *School Effectiveness and School Improvement, 3,* 69-88.

Crowson, R. L., & Porter-Gehrie, C. (1980). The discretionary behavior of principals in large-city schools. *Educational Administration Quarterly, 16,* 45-69.

Cuban, L. (1989). The district superintendent and the restructuring of schools: A realistic appraisal. In T. Sergiovanni & J. Moore (Eds.), *Schooling for tomorrow: Directing reforms to issues that count* (pp. 251-271). Boston: Allyn & Bacon.

Cunningham, L. L. (1990). Educational leadership and administration: Retrospective and prospective views. In B. Mitchell & L. L. Cunningham (Eds.), *Educational leadership and changing contexts of families, communities, and schools* (pp. 1-18). Chicago: University of Chicago Press.

Daft, R. L. (1983). *Organizational theory and design.* St. Paul: West.

Daft, R. L., Sormunen, J., & Parks, D. (1988). Chief executive scanning, environmental characteristics, and company performance: An empirical study. *Strategic Management Journal, 9,* 123-139.

Darling-Hammond, L., & Berry, B. (1988). *The evolution of teacher policy.* Santa Monica, CA: Rand.

Darling-Hammond, L., & Snyder, J. (1992). Reframing accountability: Creating learner-centered schools. In A. Lieberman (Ed.), *The changing contexts of teaching* (pp. 11-36). Chicago: University of Chicago Press.

Deal, T. E. (1987). Effective school principals: Counselors, engineers, pawnbrokers, poets . . . or instructional leaders? In W. Greenfield (Ed.), *Instructional leadership: Concepts, issues, and controversies* (pp. 230-246). Boston: Allyn & Bacon.

Dempsey, R. A. (1986). *Adolescent suicide. The trauma of adolescent suicide: A time for special leadership by principals.* Reston, VA.

Duignan, P. A. (1990). School-based decision making and management: Retrospect and prospect. In J. D. Chapman (Ed.), *School-based decision making and management* (pp. 327-345). London: Falmer.

Eberly, D. J. (1993, February). National youth service: A developing institution. *NASSP Bulletin, 77*(550), 50-57

Edmonds, R., & Fredericksen, J. R. (1978). *Search for effective schools: The identification and analysis of city schools that are instructionally effective for poor children.* Cambridge: Harvard University Center for Urban Studies.

Educational Research Service. (1985). *Evaluating administrator performance.* Arlington, VA: Author.

Elam, S. M. (1990). The 22nd annual Gallup poll of the public's attitudes toward the public schools. *Phi Delta Kappan, 72*(1), 41-55.

Elmore, R. (1990). *Comments prepared for the Reinventing School Leadership Conference.* Boston: National Center for Educational Leadership.

English, F. W., & Hill, J. C. (1990). *Restructuring: The principal and curriculum change* (Report of the NASSP Curriculum Council). Reston, VA: National Association of Secondary School Principals.

Epstein, J. L., & Connors, L. J. (1992). *School and family partnerships.* Reston, VA: National Association of Secondary School Principals.

Erlandson, D. A., & Witters-Churchill, L. J. (1990). Advances in the principalship: Performance and reflection. In P. W. Thurston & L. S. Lotto (Eds.), *Advances in Educational Administration* (Vol. 1B, pp. 121-162). Greenwich, CT: JAI.

Fallon, B. J. (1979, January). Principals are instructional leaders: Hit or myth? *NASSP Bulletin, 55*(351), 67-71.

Firestone, W. A. (1991). Merit pay and job enlargement as reforms: Incentives, implementation, and teacher response. *Educational Evaluation and Policy Analysis, 13,* 269-288.

Firestone, W. A., Fuhrman, S., & Kirst, M. W. (1990). An overview of educational reform since 1983. In J. Murphy (Ed.), *The educational reform movement of the 1980s: Perspectives and cases* (pp. 349-364). Berkeley, CA: McCutchan.

Firestone, W., & Wilson, B. (1986). Using bureaucratic and cultural linkages to improve instruction: The principal's contribution. *Educational Administration Quarterly, 21*(2), 7-30.

Fullan, M. (1982). *The meaning of educational change.* New York: Teachers College Press.

Fullan, M. (1991). *The new meaning of educational change.* New York: Teachers College Press.

Galaskiewicz, J ., & Wasserman, S. (1989). Mimetic processes within an interorganizational field: An empirical test. *Administrative Science Quarterly, 34,* 454-479.

Galbraith, J. A. (1977). *Organization design.* Reading, MA: Addison-Wesley.

Garrison, J. W. (1988). Democracy, scientific knowledge, and teacher empowerment. *Teachers College Record, 89,* 487-504.

Ginsberg, R., & Wimpelberg, R. K. (1987). Educational change by commission: Attempting "trickle down" reform. *Educational Evaluation and Policy Analysis, 9,* 344-360.

Glaser, B. G., & Strauss, A. L. (1967). *The discovery of grounded theory: Strategies for qualitative research.* Chicago: Aldine.

Glasman, N. S. (1986). *Evaluation-based leadership: School administration in contemporary perspective.* Albany: State University of New York Press.

Glasman, N. S., & Nevo, D. (1988). *Evaluation in decision making.* Boston: Kluwer Academic.

Goldring, E. B. (1986). The school community: Its effects on principals' perceptions of parents. *Educational Administration Quarterly, 22,* 115-132.

Goldring, E. B. (1987). Elementary school principals as boundary spanners: Their engagement with parents. *Journal of Educational Administration, 28,* 53-62.

Goldring, E. B. (1990). The district context and principals' sentiments towards parents. *Urban Education, 24*(4), 391-403.

Goldring, E. B. (1993). Principals, parents and administrative superiors. *Educational Administration Quarterly, 29*(1), 93-117.

Goldring, E. B., & Chen, M. (in press). Preparing empowered teachers for educational leadership positions in post-reformed schools. *Planning and Changing.*

Goldring, E., & Hallinger, P. (1992). *District control contexts and school organizational processes.* Paper presented at the annual meeting of the American Educational Research Association, San Francisco.

Goodlad, J. (1984). *A place called school.* New York: McGraw-Hill.

Goodman, J. (1987, April). *Key factors in becoming (or not becoming) an empowered elementary school teacher: A preliminary study of selected novices.* Paper presented at the annual meeting of the American Educational Research Association, Washington, DC.

Gracey, H. L. (1972). *Curriculum or craftsmanship.* Chicago: University of Chicago Press.

Greenfield, W. (1985). The moral socialization of school administrators: Informal role learning outcomes. *Educational Administration Quarterly, 21,* 99-120.

Greenfield, W. (1987). Moral imagination and interpersonal competence: Antecedents to instructional leadership. In W. Greenfield (Ed.), *Instructional Leadership* (pp. 56-73). Boston: Allyn & Bacon.

Gursky, D. (1990, March). Without principal. *Teacher Magazine, 1*(6), 56-63.

Guthrie, J. W. (1990). The evolution of educational management: Eroding myths and emerging models. In B. Mitchell & L. L.

Cunningham (Eds.), *Educational leadership and changing contexts of families, communities, and schools* (pp. 210-231). Chicago: University of Chicago Press.

Hallinger, P. (1992). School leadership development. *Education and Urban Society, 24*, 300-316.

Hallinger, P., & Hausman, C. (1993). *Radical reform for incremental change: The implementation of site-based management and shared decision-making in perspecitve.* Paper presented at the Annual Meeting of the American Educational Research Association, Atlanta, GA.

Hallinger, P., & Murphy, J. (1987). Instructional leadership in the school context. In W. Greenfield (Ed.), *Instructional leadership: Concepts, issues, and controversies* (pp. 179-203). Boston: Allyn & Bacon.

Hallinger, P., Murphy, J., & Hausman, C. (1992). Restructuring schools: Principals' perceptions of fundamental educational reform. *Educational Administration Quarterly, 28*(3), 314-329.

Hallinger, P., Murphy, J., Weil, M., Mesa, R. P., & Mitman, A. (1983, May). Identifying the specific practices, behaviors for principals. *NASSP Bulletin, 67*(643), 83-91.

Hallinger, P., & Richardson, D. (1988). Models of shared leadership: Evolving structures and relationships. *Urban Review, 20*, 226-244.

Hallinger, P., & Wimpleberg, R. (1991). *New settings and changing norms for principal development* (Occasional Paper, No. 6). Boston: The National Center for Educational Leadership.

Hambrick, D. C. (1981). Specialization of environmental scanning activities among upper level executives. *Journal of Management Studies, 18*, 299-320.

Hammersley, M., & Atkinson, P. (1983). *Ethnography, principles in action.* London: Tavistock.

Hannaway, J. (1989). *Managers managing: The working of an administrative system.* New York: Oxford University Press.

Hannaway, J., & Sproull, L. S. (1978). Who's running the show? Coordination and control in educational organizations. *Administrator's Notebook, 27*, 1-4.

Hart, A. W. (1987). A career ladder's effect on teacher career and work attitudes. *American Educational Research Journal, 24*(4), 479-503.

Hart, A. W. (1990). Impacts of the school social unit on teacher authority during work redesign. *American Educational Research Journal, 27,* 503-532.

Hart, A. W., & Murphy, M. J. (1990). New teachers react to redesign of teacher work. *American Journal of Education, 98*(3), 224-250.

Hawley, W. D. (1989). Policy board proposals. *School Administrator, 446,* 8-11, 14-15.

Heck, R. (1992). Principals' instructional leadership and school performance: Implications for policy development. *Educational Evaluation and Policy Analysis, 14*(1), 21-34.

Heck, R., Larsen, T., & Marcoulides, G. (1990). Instructional leadership and student achievement: Validation of a causal model. *Educational Administration Quarterly, 26*(2), 94-125.

Henderson, A. (Ed.). (1981). *Parent participation—Student achievement: The evidence grows.* Columbia, MD: National Committee for Citizens in Education.

Hollister, C. D. (1979). School bureaucratization as a response to parents' demands. *Urban Education, 14,* 221-235.

Hoover-Dempsey, K. V., Bassler, O. C., & Brissie, J. S. (1987). Parent involvement: Contributions of teacher efficacy, school socioeconomic status, and other school characteristics. *American Educational Research Journal, 24*(3), 417-435.

Howard, E. R., & Keefe, J. W. (1991). *The CASE-IMS school improvement process.* Reston, VA: National Association of Secondary School Principals.

Huberman, M., & Miles, M. B. (1984). *Innovation up close: How school improvement works.* New York: Plenum.

Jacobson, S. L., & Conway, J. A. (1990). *Educational leadership in an age of reform.* New York: Longman.

Johnson, S. M. (1989). Schoolwork and its reform. In J. Hannaway & R. Crowson (Eds.), *The politics of reforming school administration* (pp. 95-112). New York: Falmer.

Joint Committee on Standards for Educational Evaluation. (1988). *The personnel evaluation standards: How to assess systems for evaluating educators.* Newbury Park, CA: Sage.

Kelley, E. (1980). *Improving school climate*. Reston, VA: National Assocation of Secondary School Principals.

Kerchner, C. T. (1990). Bureaucratic entrepreneurship: The implications of choice for school administration. In S. Bacharach (Ed.), *Education reform: Making sense of it all* (pp. 270-281). Boston: Allyn & Bacon.

Kirst, M. W., McLaughlin, M. W., & Massell, D. (1989). *Rethinking children's policy: Implications for educational administration*. Stanford, CA: Center for Educational Research, School of Education, Stanford University.

Kolb, D. A. (1983). Problem management: Learning from experience. In S. Srivastva and Associates, (Eds.), *The executive mind* (pp. 109-143). San Francisco: Jossey-Bass.

Kotter, J. P. (1979). *Power in management*. New York: ANACOM.

Kotter, J. P. (1982). *The general managers*. New York: The Free Press.

Kretorivs, J., Farber, K., & Armaline, W. (1991). Reform from the bottom up: Empowering teachers to transform schools. *Phi Delta Kappan, 73*, 295-299.

Lee, J. (1987). Instructional leadership in a junior high school: Managing realities and creating opportunities. In W. Greenfield (Ed.), *Instructional leadership: Concepts, issues, and controversies* (pp. 77-99). Boston: Allyn & Bacon.

Leighton, M. S., & Shaw, A. (1990). *Implementing complex change in urban elementary schools*. Paper presented at the annual meeting of the American Educational Research Association, Boston.

Leithwood, K., & Jantzi, D. (1990, June). *Transformational leadership: How principals can help reform school cultures*. Paper presented at the Canadian Association for Curriculum Studies Annual Meeting, Victoria, B.C.

Leithwood, K., & Montgomery, D. (1982). The role of the elementary school principal in program improvement. *Review of Educational Research, 52*, 309-339.

Leithwood, K. A., & Steinbach, R. (in press). Indicators of transformational leadership in the everyday problem solving of school administrators. *Journal of Personnel Evaluation in Education*.

Levine, S. (1989). *Promoting adult growth in schools.* Boston: Allyn & Bacon.

Lightfoot, S. L. (1983). *The good high school.* New York: Basic.

Little, J. W. (1982). The effective principal. *American Education, 18,* 38-43.

Lortie, D. (1975). *Schoolteacher: A sociological study.* Chicago: University of Chicago Press.

Louis, K. S., & Miles, M. (1990). *Improving the urban high school.* New York: Teachers College Press.

Maeroff, G. (1988). A blueprint for empowering teachers. *Phi Delta Kappan, 69,* 472-477.

Malen, B., & Ogawa, R. T. (1988). Professional-patron influence on site-based governance councils: A confounding case study. *Educational Evaluation and Policy Analysis, 10,* 251-270.

March, J. G., & Olsen, J. P. (1976). *Ambiguity and choice in organizations.* Bergen, Norway: Universitetsforlaget.

McLaughlin, M. W. (1987). Learning from experience: Lessons from policy implementation. *Educational Evaluation and Policy Analysis, 9*(2), 171-178.

Meyer, J. W., & Rowan, B. (1975). *Notes on the structure of educational organizations: Revised version.* Paper presented at the annual meeting of the American Sociological Association, San Francisco.

Meyer, J. W., & Rowan, B. (1977). Institutionalized organizations: Formal structure as myth and ceremony. *American Journal of Sociology, 83,* 340-363.

MGT of America. (1990, August). *An evaluation of the 1988-89 principal incentive program* (Report submitted to the South Carolina State Department of Education). Tallahassee, FL: Author.

Michael, R. O., Short, P., & Greer, J. T. (1991). *Principals' perceptions of school empowerment: What we say is what we are.* Paper presented at the annual meeting of the University Council for Educational Administration, Baltimore, MD.

Morris, V. C., Crowson, R. L., Porter-Gehrie, C., & Hurwitz, E., Jr. (1984). *Principals in action: The reality of managing schools.* Columbus, OH: Merrill.

Mulkeen, T. A., & Tetenbaum, T. J. (1990). Teaching and learning in knowledge organizations: Implications for the preparation of school administrators. *Journal of Educational Administration,* *28,* 14-22.

Murphy, J. (1990a). The educational reform movement of the 1980s: A comprehensive analysis. In J. Murphy (Ed.) *The educational reform movement of the 1980s: Perspectives and cases* (pp. 3-55). Berkeley: McCutchan.

Murphy, J. (1990b). Restructuring the technical core of preparation programs in educational administration. *UCEA Review, 31,* 4-5, 10-14.

Murphy, J. (1991). *Restructuring schools: Capturing and assessing the phenomena.* New York: Teachers College Press.

Murphy, J. (1993). *The landscape of leadership preparation: Patterns and possibilities.* Newbury Park, CA: Sage.

Murphy, J., & Hallinger, P. (1986). The superintendent as instructional leader: Findings from effective school districts. *Journal of Educational Administration, 24,* 213-231.

Murphy, J., & Hallinger, P. (1992). The principalship in an era of transformation. *Journal of Educational Administration, 30*(3), 77-88.

National Association of Elementary School Principals. (1992) Alexandria, VA: NAESP.

National Commission on Excellence in Education. (1983, April). *A nation at risk: The imperative of educational reform.* Washington, DC: U.S. Government Printing Office.

National Commission on Excellence in Educational Administration. (1987). *Leaders for America's schools.* Tempe, AZ: University Council of Educational Administration.

National Governors' Association Task Force on Education (1990). *Education America: State strategies for achieving the national education goals.* Washington, DC: National Governors' Association.

Nevo, D. (1991, October). *An evaluation-minded school: Developing internal school evaluation systems.* Paper presented at the annual meeting of the American Evaluation Association, Chicago.

Orfield, G., & Monfort, F. (1988). *Racial change and desegregation in large school districts: Trends through the 1986-87 school year.* Alexandria, VA: National School Boards Association.

Pellicer, L. O. (1982, October). Providing instructional leadership: A principal challenge. *NASSP Bulletin, 66*(456), 27-31.

Peterson, K. (1984). Mechanisms of administrative control over managers in educational organizations. *Administrative Science Quarterly, 29*(4), pp. 573-597.

Peterson, K. (1985). Obstacles to learning from experience and principal training. *Urban Review, 17,* 189-200.

Peterson, K. D. (1987). Administrative control and instructional leadership. In W. Greenfield (Ed.), *Instructional leadership* (pp. 139-152). Boston: Allyn & Bacon.

Peterson, K., & Finn, C. (1985). Principals, superintendents, and the administrator's art. *The Public Interest, 79,* 42-62.

Peterson, P. E. (1976). *School politics Chicago style.* Chicago: University of Chicago Press.

Pfeffer, J. (1972). Size and composition of corporate boards of directors: The organization and its environment. *Administrative Science Quarterly, 17,* 218-228.

Pfeffer, J., & Salancik, G. (1978). *The external control of organizations.* New York: Harper & Row.

Poston, W. K., Jr. (1992, January). Shifting away from the super-principal complex. *NASSP Bulletin, 76*(540), 32-36.

Prestine, N. A. (1991, October) *Shared decision making in restructuring essential schools: The role of the principal.* Paper presented at the University Council for Educational Administration Annual Conference, Baltimore, MD.

Prestine, N. A., & LeGrand, B. F. (1991). Cognitive learning theory and the preparation of educational administrators: Implications for practice and policy. *Educational Administration Quarterly, 27,* 61-89.

Rallis, S. (1986). The myth of the "great principal." *Phi Delta Kappan, 68,* 300-304.

Rallis, S. (1988). Room at the top: Conditions for effective school leadership. *Phi Delta Kappan, 69,* 643-647.

Rallis, S. (1989). *The learning disabilities identification project: Classroom alternative process, summative evaluation report* (Technical report). Providence: Center for Evaluation and Research, Rhode Island Department of Education.

Rallis, S. (1990). Professional teachers and restructured schools: Leadership challenges. In B. Mitchell & L. L. Cunningham (Eds.),

Educational leadership and changing contexts of families, communities, and schools (pp. 184-209). Chicago: University of Chicago Press.

Rallis, S. (1991). *Principals' perspectives on the least restrictive environment initiative.* Unpublished summary report. Providence: Center for Evaluation and Research, Rhode Island College.

Rallis, S. F. (1992). *Portrait of leadership: Connecting the conversations about change* (Monograph for the Coalition of Essential Schools). Providence, RI: Brown University.

Rallis, S. F., & Phleger, J. M. (1990, April). *Contextual variables for program success: Describing impact of goal achievement.* Paper presented at the annual meeting of the American Educational Research Association, Boston, MA.

Rhodes, L. A. (1988, August). *Technology as a leadership tool.* Paper presented at the Small School District and Rural District Forum Summer Conference, American Association of School Administrators, Brainerd, MN.

Richardson, M. D. (1988, June). The administrative assessment center: An opportunity for service. Paper presented at the Annual Meeting of the Kentucky Association of School Superintendents, Louisville.

Rizvi, F. (1990). Horizontal accountability. In J. D. Chapman (Ed.), *School-based decision-making and management* (pp. 299-324). London: Falmer.

Roberts, L. (1990). *School leadership for the 1990s: One very personal vision.* Paper presented at the Reinventing School Leadership Conference, National Center for Educational Leadership, Boston.

Rosenholtz, S. (1985). Effective schools: Interpreting the evidence. *American Journal of Education, 93,* 352-388.

Schmitt, N., & Doherty, M. (1988). *NASSP study of measurement and model linkage issues for the Comprehensive Assessment of School Environment* (Technical report). East Lansing: Michigan State University.

Schon, D. (1983). *The reflective practitioner: How professionals think in action.* New York: Basic Books.

Schulman, L. S. (1988). A union of insufficiencies: Strategies for teacher assessment in a period of educational reform. *Educational Leadership, 46*(3), 36-41.

Scott, W. R. (1981). *Organizations, rational, natural and open systems.* Englewood Cliffs, NJ: Prentice-Hall.

Scriven, M. (1967). The methodology of evaluation. In R. W. Tyler, R. M. Gagne, & M. Scriven (Eds.), *Perspectives of curriculum evaluation* (AERA Monograph Series on Curriculum Evaluation No. 1, pp. 39-84). Chicago: Rand McNally.

Seeley, D., Niermeyer, J., & Greenspan, R. (1990, May). *Principals speak on restructuring and school leadership* (Report No. 1). New York: Principals Speak Project, CUNY.

Shedd, J. B., & Bacharach, S. B. (1991). *Tangled hierarchies: Teachers as professionals and the management of schools.* San Francisco: Jossey-Bass..

Sickler, J. (1988). Teachers in charge: Empowering the professionals. *Phi Delta Kappan, 69,* 354-376.

Silver, P. F. (1987). The Center for Advancing Principalship Excellence (APEX): An approach to professionalizing educational administration. In J. Murphy & P. Hallinger (Eds.), *Approaches to administrative training in education* (pp. 67-82). Albany: SUNY Press.

Sizer, T. R. (1984). *Horace's compromise: The dilemma of the American high school.* Boston: Houghton Mifflin.

Sizer, T. R. (1992). *Horace's school: Redesigning the American high school.* New York: Houghton Mifflin.

Slater, R. O., & Doig, J. W. (1988). Leadership in education: Issues of entrepreneurship and environment. *Education and Urban Society, 20,* 294-301.

Smylie, M. (1992). Teacher participation in school decision making: Assessing willingness to participate. *Educational Evaluation and Policy Analysis, 14,* 53-67.

Snyder, K., & Johnson, W. (1985). Retraining principals for productive school management. *Educational Research Quarterly, 9,* 19-27.

Sparks, D. (1992, June 10). 13 tips for managing change. *Education Week,* p. 22.

Spradley, J. P. (1979). *The ethnographic interview.* New York: Holt, Rinehart, & Winston.

Steffy, B. E. (1990). *Can rational organizational models really reform anything?* Paper presented at the annual meeting of the University Council on Educational Administration, Pittsburgh.

Taylor, E. E. (1991). Implementing school-based governance. *Schools in the Middle, 1*(12), 23-25.

Tennessee State Board of Education. (1990, November). *Master plan for Tennessee schools: Preparing for the twentieth century.* Nashville: Author.

Thompson, J. D. (1967). *Organizations in action.* New York: McGraw-Hill.

Tom, A. (1985). Inquiring into inquiry-oriented teacher education. *Journal of Education, 36,* 35-44.

Underwood, J. (1990). State legislative responses to educational reform literature. In P. W. Thurston & L. S. Lotto (Eds.), *Recent advances in educational administration* (Vol. 1A, pp. 139-175). Greenwich, CT: JAI.

United States Department of Education, National Center of Education Statistics. (1984). *High school and beyond: Administration and teacher survey.* Washington, DC: Office of Educational Research and Improvement, USDE.

United States Department of Education. (1988). *Tenth annual report to Congress on the implementation of the Education of the Handicapped Act.* Washington, DC: Author.

United States Department of Education. (1989). *Eleventh annual report to Congress on the implementation of the Education of the Handicapped Act.* Washington, DC: Author.

United States Department of Education. (1990). *Twelfth annual report to Congress of the implementation of the Education of the Handicapped Act.* Washington, DC: Author.

Vidich, A., & Bensman, J. (1960). *Small town in mass society.* New York: Doubleday.

Wasley, P. (1991, Fall). Stirring the chalkdust: Practices in essential schools. *Teachers College Record, 93*(1), 28-42.

Weick, K. (1976). Educational organizations as loosely coupled systems. *Administrative Science Quarterly, 21,* 1-16.

Wick, J. W. (1987). *School-based evaluation.* Boston: Kluwer Academic.

Wimpleberg, R. K. (1987). The dilemma of instructional leadership and a central role for central office. In W. Greenfield (Ed.), *Instructional Leadership* (pp. 100-117). Newton, MA: Allyn & Bacon.

Wimpleberg, R. K. (1990). The inservice development of principals. In P. W. Thurston & L. S. Lotto (Eds.), *Advances in Educational Administration*, (Vol. 1B, pp. 73-119). Greenwich, CT: JAI.

Wolcott, H. F. (1973). *The man in the principal's office*. New York: Holt, Rinehart & Winston.

Wolf, E. (1988). The school superintendent in the reform era: Perceptions of practitioners, principals, and pundits. *Peabody Journal of Education, 65*, 9-30.

Wolf, K. (1991). The schoolteacher's portfolio: Issues in design, implementation, and evaluation. *Phi Delta Kappan, 73*, 129-136.

Index